LOVE, HONOUR AND ANNOY

A humorous memoir about
growing old together

Sarah Catherine Knights

Sarah Knights

Copyright © 2024 Sarah Catherine Knights

All rights reserved

The characters and events portrayed in this book are not fictitious. Any similarity to real persons, living or dead, is intended by the author.

No part of this book may be reproduced, or stored in a retrieval system, or transmitted in any form or by any means, electronic, mechanical, photocopying, recording, or otherwise, without express written permission of the publisher.

This book is dedicated to Peter – who else? Thank you for putting up with me for so long ... and thank you for letting me write about you. You said you didn't mind me taking the mickey, so I did ... relentlessly.

CONTENTS

Title Page
Copyright
Dedication
Chapter 1 | 1
Chapter 2 | 5
Chapter 3 | 41
Chapter 4 | 55
Chapter 5 | 73
Chapter 6 | 89
Chapter 7 | 99
Chapter 8 | 107
Chapter 9 | 123
Chapter 10 | 131
Chapter 11 | 136
Chapter 12 | 141
Chapter 13 | 150
Chapter 14 | 169

Chapter 15	178
Chapter 16	185
Chapter 17	197
Chapter 18	211
Books By This Author	221
About The Author	229

CHAPTER 1

"I love being married. It's so great to find that one special person you want to annoy for the rest of your life." —Rita Rudner

Two Unlikely People Get Together

Two people meet in 1970 and are destined to spend their entire life together.

How on earth does that work?

Our two elderly protagonists, that is, me and him, are the most unlikely couple. On paper, we have nothing in common.

He grew up in Wembley, London; I grew up in the depths of the English countryside. I went to a posh girls' private school; he went to a boys' grammar. Ironically, his parents were well off and my divorced mum had no money – I will explain the *posh school* later. His parents were very happily married, mine divorced acrimoniously. He was a bit of a maths genius, I was an English aficionado. He was heavily into sport ... and I definitely wasn't. I *had* been sporty at school, but by the time we met, most of my enthusiasm had waned. I was, however, into riding horses: his attitude to them was that, *'they bite at one end and kick at the other.'* He'd travelled all over the world. I'd been virtually nowhere (except for a period just before my parents split up, when we went to live in Denmark). I was a bit of an academic nerd, when it came to school/university study; he did as little as possible and got chucked out of two universities. I loved dogs, he didn't. In fact, he was scared stiff of them, which our family dog latched onto straightaway and made it its mission to frighten him witless every time he came to see me. I'm surprised it didn't put him off me, to be honest. I loved music and he definitely didn't. Benny Hill's *Ernie, The Fastest Milkman in the West* and The Bonzo Dog Doo-Dah Band's *The Intro and the Outro,* were the sum total of his popular musical knowledge.

How *did* these two polar opposites meet, marry and stay together for over fifty years? Yes, FIFTY. It's a mystery and a bloody miracle, even to *me* ... and I'm living it, but I'm going to try to explain in the following pages.

So, there have been fifty years, half a century or 18,250 days of life together ... a glorious mix of bickering, laughing, arguing, crying, shouting, silence, apologies, forgiveness, seething resentment, tearful making up and ultimately, love. Oh ... and being incredibly annoyed with each other, a lot of the time. All of this, interspersed, along the way, with the arrival of three amazing children, four dogs, three cats, two horses, old bangers that broke down all the time, married quarters, four of our own houses and multiple moves: to Scotland, Lincolnshire, Wiltshire, Cyprus and back to Wiltshire.

I look back and can't believe all the things that have happened to us. It's a cliché to say *time goes quickly*, we all know that, but it's scary to think we may only have ten good years left on this wonderful planet. None of us know when we're leaving it and I know I've been incredibly lucky to lead a happy, charmed life in a fantastic part of the globe. So ... I thought that before I lose the ability to remember who I am and why I'm here, I wanted to make sense of my life, if that's even possible.

Once, I used to think people of seventy were well and truly past it, but when you get here, you realise seventy year olds are just people with saggier skin. Inside, we are who we've always been and we've had a life, crammed full of love, drama, tragedy and laughs, that might be worth writing about.

If people read this, that's amazing, but I've thoroughly enjoyed simply 'getting it down'. It's stirred memories and emotions that had been filed away for a long time; it's made me nostalgic for the past, thankful for the present and a little bit scared of the future.

There's something intrinsically sad and very *unfunny* about where we are in life: decrepitude, aging, empty nest and downsizing, so I wanted to look at it with a different perspective and hopefully make something humorous ... because life's always better if you can see the funny side.

CHAPTER 2

"Look, you want to know what marriage is really like? Fine. You wake up, she's there. You come back from work, she's there. You fall asleep, she's there. You eat dinner, she's there. You know? I mean, I know that sounds like a bad thing, but it's not." —Ray Romano as Ray Barone on Everybody Loves Raymond

A Day In The Life Of Us – February, 2022

I bought a bunch of daffodils yesterday to cheer myself up, hoping that spring is peeking around the proverbial corner. They're now sitting smugly on the kitchen table, fully open, smiling from their vase, as if to say, this is as good as it gets; there's a *long* way to go till Spring. So yellow, so happy ... so annoyingly *upbeat* in their appearance. The wind is roaring down the chimney, making the house feel as if it's being invaded by an alien force, over which I have no control. Outside, I can see next door's tree swaying precariously, buffeted by sudden gusts; its branches are far too near our roof, for my liking. This is the third day of the storms and there seems to be no let up. Flooding and building damage is on the news every day, so I suppose we're lucky in this part of the country, with only minor problems, like fences falling down, muddy fields and diversions.

Today, I decided to start writing a memoir, as I have an endless amount of time to fill and plenty of things to say. A memoir is a bit like an autobiography, but it's written around a theme. My theme is: our very (very) long marriage. Inevitably, you end up thinking about how on earth you've got to be so old. I don't *feel* seventy and hopefully, don't look it (although other opinions may vary); in the not too distant past, I would have been sitting in my bath chair, dribbling in a corner by now. Fortunately, with modern nutrition, seventy is the new fifty; you see some glamorous ladies of my age around. I'm not saying *I'm* one, but I'm active: walking twice a day with my dog, swimming twice a week in the pool and surfing in the waves of Cornwall, when I can. I even did a plank this morning and held it for quite a decent time.

I could sit down, put my feet up and quietly fall into being old, but I'm determined not to. As long as can, I want to carry on as if I'm young. Fortunately, I'm healthy and as long as I am, I'm going to be like one of those face creams they advertise: I'm going *to fight the visible signs of ageing*. I've got all my faculties, can walk in a straight line, talk without spitting out false teeth and I know who the Prime Minister is (although recently, with the rapid turnaround, that's been rather more challenging).

I see my three children as often as possible; they've all got busy lives in distant places but we're always FaceTiming, sending WhatsApp messages and even simply phoning each other. Exciting things happen to them every day, so I absorb their lives and live vicariously. I can still remember how it feels to be so busy with life each day, that weeks pass without even *thinking* about how other people might be getting on.

Peter, my partner of half a century, is here in the house, somewhere, padding around. He's probably upstairs in his 'office' sitting at his desk, doing Wordle. He sends me clues on Whatsapp which, I tell him every day, only make sense when I've actually found the word myself.

So ... how *do* we fill our time?

When the house doesn't demand our attention, Peter plays tennis or golf, wrestles with advanced Suduko and reads 'The Times' from cover to cover. Well, not the actual paper, as he's attached to his iPad like a limpet to a rock, these days. Very modern. When he's watching TV and 'playing on his iPad', as I call it, I say, *'It's like living with a teenager'.* He counters by saying that I'm worse, which I suppose is true: my iPhone's my entire life. I'd cease to exist without it. (Did you know there's a new word for constantly looking at your phone/iPad when you're with someone else? It's called *Phubbing:* snubbing another person by constantly using your smartphone. We do it on a daily basis).

So that's us – we live in the same house, breathe the same air, read the same news on our apps and 'vigorously exchange views' when we can be bothered. These days, however, I know all his views and can't really raise much enthusiasm for exchanging his, with mine; I know all mine too. *Mine* are basically that I don't have many strong opinions any more (except my hatred of Trump) and *his* are, that it's worth getting apoplectic about just about *everything*. I'm not sure why he's not Chancellor of the Exchequer; he's far more knowledgeable than all of them, past and present incumbents, put together. My general view is: what's the point of getting worked up about Boris, Brexit or Rishi? The country voted for them all, so we've only got ourselves to blame. It just gives me higher blood pressure than I've already got and gets me in a really bad mood. So, when Peter starts on one of his rants, I've learned to switch off and say something like, "*Why don't you become an MP, if you're so concerned about it?*" which I know will wind him up, as it's the last thing he'd ever do. Or, I simply walk out of the house with my four-legged friend.

I forgot to mention the other person who hangs out in this house, which is disgraceful, as she's the only one who adds a bit fun to our rather empty nest. With her four legs, long tail, brown eyes, cold, wet nose and ears that flap in the wind, you can tell she's not *technically* a person, but she's more human than a lot of the population and frankly, a lot nicer. She has an insatiable appetite that can never be satisfied; her whole existence revolves around her next 'treat'. Treats are for doing something good, but she only has to *exist* to get one from us. She's always so ecstatic to see me (and annoyingly, any other person, for that matter) but she makes me feel special, for a moment. She's even pleased to see Peter, which is more than I can say for myself. *Ha ha*, I don't mean it. I love my husband, I do, but after fifty years of him, I can't profess to being excited every time he walks in the room, whereas Mabel can. She jumps up, she wags, she licks ... 'if only you were that pleased to see me,' Peter says, 'our sex life would take on a whole new perspective'. Mabel's standing by me right now, as I type, ready for action.

Why am I writing about our life? I'm not sure. Maybe because I'm bored stupid and am trying to fill my time, or *maybe* because I want to record something for posterity, to make me feel as if my life on this planet was for *some* reason ... but for the life of me, I can't work out what it is. As you get older, it seems more and more likely that there was no point to any of it, *whatsoever*. I feel as if I'm rushing towards oblivion and of course, I am. We all are, aren't we? So, writing something serves two purposes: firstly, it makes me look busy and Peter doesn't interfere with me and suggest we sort out the airing cupboard or something equally riveting and secondly, *maybe*, someone will read this in the future and think about us, just a little bit.

Mabel has now given up looking enthusiastic and has slumped down on the floor with her back to me. She's in a huff. She was convinced that I was just about to take her for a walk and I've let her down, *again*. I got up at 7.30 and made us tea, let her out into the garden for a pee and then she rushed in to consume her kibble, a polite word for dried food 'packed with goodness' which looks more like rabbit droppings to me, than nutritious food. Actually, on reflection, maybe that's why she likes them: any shit, and I mean *any*, is gratefully received.

She then rushed up to our bed to lick Peter awake and settled down between us, until we deigned to get up; she's been hoping for a walk ever since. Unfortunately for her, she's landed with two old humans who have nothing better to do than languish in bed until nine a.m. most days. No early morning walks, no toddler food to eat off the floor, no dirty nappies to steal and chew. It's just tedium from morning till night, with a break for two long walks. Yes, Mabel, you do rather well ... if you'd been with me when the kids were growing up, you'd have been at the bottom of the pecking order and been flung in the car for the shortest possible walk ... so there are *some* advantages to living with a couple of old codgers.

#

I've just got back in from her walk. She persuaded me to get off my arse in the end, by staring directly at me for at least ten minutes and jumping up every time I moved. It shows how often I'm on my phone, as Mabel now assumes the magnetic *click* when I close my phone case, means I'm *actually* going to do something constructive which in her eyes, is to go out for a walk and dedicate my entire existence to throwing a ball.

It's like living on your own: the house, on my return, is in exactly the same state as when I left it. Nothing has moved or stirred. Peter's probably *still* upstairs in his office doing a very important maths game, as we speak. Best not disturb.

The walk was muddy and windy, as they always are at this time of year. February really is the pits. Nothing going for it at all. We can pretend Spring is nearly here, but it *really* isn't. Any poor flowers that try to push through, like snowdrops, are shaken by the wind and coshed over the head with flying debris. Still, Mabel enjoyed herself. She pulled me down the hill, careered off across the field once we got there, dipped into the river for a wild swim, chased a few crows, terrorised a small terrier and nearly took my fingers off when I gave her a treat. I've given up saying *'gently'* when I give her a treat; the concept isn't one that she grasps easily. She doesn't mean to hurt me, but her eagerness to get the rather disgusting looking strip of chemicals, gets the better of her, every time. I call it 'gentle snatching' – a new expression I've invented that sums up her decisive, yet brutal, assault on my fingers. She starts off with good intentions, but then grabs the treat with her teeth, in case it's whisked away from her. I haven't mentioned that she's only two, so she's still learning to be nice.

On the walk, she found one of the best sticks she's ever found – straight, long and unbreakable (her words, not mine). She carried it loyally for the whole walk, as if her life depended on it, only to abandon it mercilessly, minutes before getting home. It now lies on the pavement, waiting to trip up the next pensioner. Having spent at least half an hour on grass in fields on her walk, she then decided to relieve herself on the pavement, going back up the road. Delightful. This is one aspect of dogs I'm not so fond of: putting one's hand into a plastic bag and picking up warm, steaming poo and attempting to tie a knot in said bag, without getting said shit on one's hands. It's an absolute delight. When did this *'please pick up your poo'* lark start? In the good old days, pre-poo bags, pre-social conscience, poo was left to ingratiate itself into other people's shoes quite happily. Now, if I haven't got a poo bag in my pocket, it's like leaving my glasses or keys behind. 'Have you got the poo bags?' Peter yells, as we leave the house to go the local theatre. Ha Ha. Bit of an exaggeration … but you know what I mean. One little trick I've discovered with poo on the pavement (sounds like a song title to me – Adele, you missed a trick there with *Chasing Pavements*) is to pick up some old leaves/debris first and then the poo. This helps get it all in there and any smears can be covered over with leaves. This is assuming there are leaves around at the right moment, I know, but I like to pass on little tips when it comes to dealing with dog poo. Having picked it up, I then finish the walk with the 'bag of shame' dangling from my fingers, until I can get to the poo bin, waiting *shitily* at the end of the road. How I love to open the top of the bin and fling in my donation. I can't help but feel sorry for the person whose job it is to collect dog poo from bins. I bet they can't wait to start each day.

As you can see, my life is full of adventures – I can't believe I've just spent a whole paragraph describing how to pick up dog poo. Has my life *really* come to this?

Yes it has.

So … that's been my morning so far.

#

The afternoon that same day, begins on a sour note. We both need to do some 'life admin '(God, how I hate that term) and this involves a lot of swearing on Peter's part … and quiet seething on mine. I was getting on with ordering some theatre tickets, writing a couple of emails and making a doctor's appointment, when I heard him explode with anger.

"For FUCK'S SAKE … I'm going round in sodding circles here. They tell me I've got to log in and when I do, they tell me I'm using the wrong password and then when I try to change the password, they tell me I've already used it or it needs eight letters, a symbol *and* a number and my inside leg measurement. *For crying out loud."*

This is the sort of thing that happens every time Peter does anything on a computer; it's as if there's a conspiracy *'out there* ' that is deliberately designed to piss him off. Every website has special rules for him and him alone, which change *just* before he tries to log on. He's convinced that people *'change the system'* without thinking of the consequences for innocent people like him, who just want to *'look at my own sodding account'* ... *'pay a bloody bill'* etc. etc.

It's the same with phone calls – you know the kind – where you're kept waiting for half an hour, when they tell you how *important* you are to them and that you're only *thirteenth* in the queue. When Peter is on this type of call, he puts them on speaker, so that he can be even more annoyed by the crappy music they use to entertain you while you're waiting. When the music is interrupted by a recorded message, to tell you how you're *still* really important to them but how much easier it would be if you went *online* to sort your problem out, he glowers at the phone, saying things like, "I can't get into my fucking account, you *arsehole*. If you hadn't locked me out of my account, I wouldn't have to be listening to this *bollocks*." It's so relaxing to listen to. When he does eventually get through, I'm usually cringing in the background, mouthing at him to remember that the poor woman on the end of the phone didn't design the software. I vacate the room when he gets to the *'I want to speak to your superior'* part of the conversation. The other day, I went for a good forty-minute dog walk and he was still on the phone to BT when I returned. I actually felt sorry for the poor person at the end of the phone, who probably went home crying that night.

Anyway, after technically slamming the phone down (unfortunately you can't do that any more with mobile phones, you can only touch the red button with total hatred) and swearing to *leave* whatever company he was dealing with (anything ranging from insurance companies, banks, car-leasing or utilities), he usually calms down a bit, but you can tell it wouldn't take much for him to start up again, so I stay well clear.

After ending a particularly fraught call, he wanders into the kitchen and I offer to make him a coffee. This afternoon, however, he suggests we go for another walk.

"Oh, okay," I said. "Are you sure?" I felt that going for a walk after an hour of life admin might not be so relaxing, for me, anyway. "I'm happy to take her on my own." Mabel, at the mere mention of the word *walk,* is already by the door, ball in mouth, tail wagging.

"No, I'll come, I could do with the fresh air," he said, "after talking to that total *wanker* for the last hour." I wonder what he thought of *you,* I wanted to add, but thought better of it.

He then proceeds to get ready. This involves putting on his walking boots which takes, on average, about an hour. Slight exaggeration, but that's how it feels. He's never been flexible and bending down to force his feet into the boots is painful to watch. Slightly along the lines of computers and phone calls, the boots have been deliberately designed to actually stop him getting his feet in them, apparently. He'd make a good conspiracy theorist.

"Poo bags?" he said.

"Yes, about a million in each pocket," I said, exaggerating slightly.

"Treats?" asked Mabel.

"Yes, about a million in each pocket," I replied and she looked distinctly relieved.

We proceed down the drive and at the bottom, I say, "Left or right?"

"God, the excitement," says Peter. "Let's go mad and go left, for a change."

Peter's walks always involve cake. This might seem strange as we live in the country and we're not particularly near shops, but whichever route we take, we always manage to slip by one of our three coffee shops. Going left, is ostensibly going in the wrong direction for the cafés, but you can do a big circle and end up conveniently walking up the town's high street.

So we set off, grey sky menacing, crows cawing in the trees, Mabel panting with anticipation and we trudge along the road, past the house having an extension, past the fill-in houses that have been crammed in the garden of one house, past the brand new square, white houses which would look more in keeping on Manly Beach and up the public right of way, that takes us through a farm and down a muddy track. By now, Mabel is off the lead and obsessively chasing her ball that Peter throws at regular intervals, but not regular enough, as far as Mabel's concerned.

We talk a bit, even laugh, but mainly we just walk; listening to the songs of hidden birds, watching rabbits scampering away unnoticed by Mabel, looking up at distant trails in the sky. We walk, hand in hand, for a while, like a couple of teenagers but then the path narrows and we walk in single file. I breathe in the country air, enjoying the exercise. We pass the llamas and the horses, spread out in the large field and then amble down the track that takes us past the wonderful views of the town, the clock tower appearing to move round the abbey as the perspective changes. We walk through a little estate and down to the river, over the bridge where the water gushes and then onto the main road through the ancient town. It's steep and we both visibly slow our pace and Mabel, now back on the lead, isn't pulling any more; she's expended her energy and is more content to walk normally.

"Do you fancy a coffee?" Peter says.

"Yea, why not?" I say, as if the thought hadn't occurred to me. Mabel knows exactly where to go these days. It's as if she too wants a coffee, or is it the cake she knows she'll share? She takes us directly to the door of the café.

"What do you want? My treat," I say, generously.

"A flat white ... and while you're there, a piece of coffee and walnut cake would be nice."

"For God's sake, I thought you were trying to eat less?"

"Well, I didn't have much for lunch ... I'll go and find a seat."

This conversation happens *literally* every time we go for a coffee.

I queue up; the young guy behind the counter with the man-bun makes polite conversation and I feel old, as I think, *What a nice young man.* In my head, I look the same as I always have, but I'm sure, to him, he thinks, *Nice old woman.* Or maybe not. I try to show him that I'm very modern, as I fumble with Apple Pay. *That'll show you, young man. I'm not as decrepit as I look. I can use technology.*

"You didn't want any cake, then?" Peter asks, as I sit down.

"I thought I'd share some of yours?"

"That wasn't the idea," he says, a bit miffed. "It's all mine ... and hers," pointing to his four-legged girlfriend, who looks on knowingly.

"Charming."

"Oh, go on then," and he takes a tiny crumb and puts it on my open hand.

He's done this joke so many times, you'd think it would get on my wick, but I still find it funny.

I often find I make friends with people in cafés if they've got a dog, much to Peter's disgust; he doesn't believe in making conversation with strangers. Dog owners are in a secret club which means that you can strike up a random conversation with them and nobody thinks you're weird. As your dog tries to smell the bottom of another dog sitting near, it's quite legitimate to say, "Aww, aren't they funny? What's his name?" and then you end up getting a potted history of the dog's life, his age, habits and sexual orientation … well, not quite, but you know what I mean.

Next to us in the café this time, is another Lab and a family of four. Mum is trying to breastfeed, toddler is running around, Dad is in the queue and Dog is causing havoc, trying to make friends with Mabel. Their dog is tied to a chair which begins to move, which frightens the dog, who then pulls even more and the chair falls over. Chaos ensues, I jump up and rescue the dog, as Mum is rather occupied.

"Thanks," she says. "He's a nutter."

"No probs," I say, trying to get the chair upright. Meanwhile, Peter is simply stuffing his face, ignoring everyone and everything. Mabel is sitting in a goody two-shoes manner, showing off.

"You've got your hands full," I say, unhelpfully.

"Yes, Mike said a dog wouldn't make much difference …"

"When you've got kids, you might as well have a dog too," I said, remembering just how *untrue* that actually was.

Mike came back to the table, carrying toasted sandwiches and sat down. The toddler sat on his lap and the baby started crying, as Mum covered up. They closed in as a family and I turned back to our table. Mabel lay down and order was (kind of) restored.

I sat, thinking of times in the past when children and dogs were a permanent fixture in our lives; I felt nostalgic for the sheer busyness of those times, when every minute of every day was taken up by other people's needs. There was no time to dwell on your own thoughts; there was too much noise, too much activity for anything to penetrate the brain. Life was fulfilling, exciting and full of hope for the future. Now, our lives suddenly felt empty and aimless, but I had to admit to myself, slightly quieter and more relaxing.

I turned to watch Peter scrolling through his phone. I got mine out, scrolled pointlessly for a few seconds and then, coming to my senses said, "Shall we go now? Seems a bit stupid, sitting here looking at our phones."

"Just checking the sport … India are 230 for 6."

"Really? That's *incredible*."

"No need to be sarcastic. It's very important. They could win the ..."

"Right, I'm off."

I stood up, lifting my muddy coat off the floor where unbeknownst to me, it had fallen and Mabel had commandeered it as a bed. Once I'd put it on, I looked down at myself admiringly: mud-laden boots, mud-splattered, dog-hair-covered coat, old black gloves that didn't quite match and a scarf that was given to me, which was far too long. Quite the fashion icon. Still, who was I trying to impress?

No one, evidently.

"I'll see you outside the Co-op. I'm going in to get some bananas and milk," I said, as Peter continued to ignore me.

"Okay," he muttered, not looking up. "I'll keep Mabel."

I nodded at the family with the dog and the woman smiled wanly. She was either looking at me with pity, as I was so blatantly being ignored by my partner, or perhaps she was smiling with envy at my ability to just get up and walk out, without any thought. Or maybe she was admiring my attire? I couldn't work out which, but I remembered the chaos when trying to go anywhere with children; it would probably take her at least ten minutes to extricate herself, having no doubt changed the baby's nappy first and taken the toddler for a wee, rescued endless items from the floor, put the baby back in the pram, loaded the pram etc etc. Maybe Mike was a modern dad and actually helped?

"Enjoy the rest of your walk," she said.

"And you," I said.

Two women, at such different times of their lives, battling on.

"See you in five," I said to my husband, who continued to ignore me. The cricket must be riveting.

I walked across the street and into the Co-op. This is a strange version of a supermarket: all the essentials, but never what you *actually* need. The box where the bananas obviously used to be was empty, so, as if apples were a good substitute, I got six wizened Gala apples, instead. Miraculously, there *was* still milk and with my bounty, I went to join the queue. For a shop that doesn't offer much in the way of produce, it does a steady trade and I seemed to have got behind the slowest queue *ever*. The woman who was at the head of the queue was buying lottery tickets, cigarettes and scratch cards, which was turning out to be a difficult ask for the new cashier and she had to ring for assistance. Having sorted that, the next person had what appeared to be, their entire week's shop; then there was the guy with just six cans of beer and finally, the young mum with a screaming child. Oh the joys. By the time it got to me, I was seriously thinking of putting my stuff back on the shelves and shooting myself.

My walking companions were standing outside when I emerged, looking impatient. Mabel was saying hello to each person who walked by, as if she was a professional greeter: *Welcome to my part of the pavement ... so glad you could come by ...* and Peter was standing there, wearing his sunglasses, despite the grey skies, ignoring her.

"God, that was painful," I said. "Remind me never to run out of anything *ever* again."

"Yea, you took your time," he said, as if I'd deliberately stayed in the shop longer than was necessary.

"Who ARE all these people who shop here? Why don't they go somewhere better and less expensive?"

"Probably for the same reason you went – they just wanted a quick shop."

"Well, that worked out well, didn't it? Why *are* you wearing sunglasses, by the way?"

"Forecast is for the sun to come out, some time today. Thought I'd be prepared."

"Oh right. Good thinking."

Again, this conversation has been had many times before. Peter's sunglasses 'thing' is an on-going joke. I think *he* thinks he looks cool and I have to admit, they DO suit him. Aviator shades, in memory of his glorious past. Not that he was a fighter pilot, but

Air Force navigator comes pretty close. Yes, his life was in flying; mine was in teaching. We actually had *lives* before we drifted around doing *sod all*. We had children, dogs, parties, jobs ... we were people with full lives: schools, holidays, ambitions, plans, finances, summer balls.

Now ... what do we do?

Walk the dog, eat cake and watch TV.

#

We stagger home, taking a different route, so that Mabel gets a different perspective, but to be honest, I think I'm giving her more imagination than she actually has. In truth, we hope we've conned her into thinking she's had two walks, the coffee stop in the middle of our walk, acting as the dividing line. Maybe she's not as stupid as we think and knows she's been conned. She couldn't care less what the landscape is like when you throw the ball, as long as you do it. She doesn't exactly look at the view of the town across the river, as I do. It's beautiful: wildebeest charging over rolling verdant vistas, waterfalls cascading over cliffs and vultures circling overhead ... not quite, I'm letting my imagination run away with me. It's more like something out of *Farming Today*: fields with rickety stiles at the fence; the river flowing fast over stones and under the bridge, leading your eye to the town above, which meanders in a haphazard way along the ridge, stone houses intermingled with brick red, yellow, and cream buildings. The abbey dominates, casting its eye over the narrow streets and remembering the time when a monk tried to fly off its ramparts.

We're standing on the bridge while Mabel has her usual tootle around the shallows, picking up the odd stone, trying to find a lost ball or simply enjoying the water.

"Do you remember when the kids were young, the way they always wanted to bring buckets and they'd wade around looking for fish?" I said, seeing them in my mind's eye.

"Yes," said Peter, "walks took forever in those days and we'd end up bringing home some poor, unsuspecting creature, who'd die almost instantly."

"Poor things … one minute you're innocently enjoying a swim and the next, you're in a bucket being held by a child, who's just as likely to drop the bucket, at any minute." A bit like life, really.

"Come on Mabel, it's time to go home." We all walk companionably back across the field, climbing over the stile more slowly than in the past; Peter spends ages lifting his leg over the stile, complaining that they're higher than they used to be. I'm not sure that's the case; Peter's joints are beginning to cause a bit of gip and the truth is, he can't lift his leg up like he used to. I must try to get him to go and see the doctor – the likelihood of *that* is nearly zilch though, as doctors are another group of professionals who, he believes, don't know what they're talking about.

"What's for supper?" he asks, as we take off our coats, back home.

"No idea."

"I thought you said we had some steak?"

"Yes, I think we have. I'll dig it out of the fridge and check the use-by date. It's been in there a while."

"It'll be fine ...". Peter is prepared to eat anything; he doesn't believe in use-by/sell-by dates. As long as it doesn't smell too bad, he'll eat it; he has the constitution of a ravenous hyena. Neither of us believe in wasting food and often eat leftovers that have been sitting in the fridge for days. I draw the line, however, at actual fur growing on things but Peter's been known to scrape it off. "Waste not, want not," is his byword. I've actually witnessed him balancing an open tomato ketchup bottle upside down on another one, making sure that every last drip is consumed.

Another thing he always says about food is, "You never know where your next meal's coming from." This is an excuse for him to eat anything that comes his way. "RAF training," he says, religiously, with a smile. It might have been true when he was on operations, but can hardly be used as a reason these days.

Does anyone else think that food and drink is *everywhere* these days? It seems that people can't walk from A to B without carrying a cup of coffee or buying a doughnut. When I was a child, back in the mists of time, we never went out for meals, *ever*. My mother couldn't afford it, but I don't think it was the done thing, anyway. We lived in the Surrey countryside and there just weren't places to eat. I'm sure if I went back to my old village today, there'd be a coffee shop on the village green, a bakery selling takeaway croissants and a fast food van parked up, selling burgers. Now, the whole population eats and drinks seemingly *all* day. It really brought it home to me when I was walking round Badminton cross-country course. (Very posh, I know, but this serves as an example, not as an indication of my Hooray Henry country life). In the past, there would have been a couple of stalls at the start, but now, there's a fast food joint at *every* jump. Can't people survive even a short walk between fences, without fainting with hunger? This sounds such an upper-class example of over-eating … staggering around a cross-country course … but it would be the same at any event now, from music festivals to rugby matches to go-karting – there would be ubiquitous food. *We,* however, can't talk, as evidenced from the fact that we can't even seem to go for a dog walk without eating, either. But that's the point, *everyone* does it now and it's filtered down to children who can't get from one meal to the next, without at least two snack breaks.

But back to supper. I grab the steak and we're in time, it's still in date … just. Peter slopes off to watch TV in the sitting room and I dutifully prepare the meal. Hardly a gastronomic delight: steak flung in the frying pan, potatoes thrown in some boiling water and a salad, chucked in a bowl. I sound like Jamie Oliver with his cockney-lad language, but I'm sure his results are somewhat better than mine. No doubt he'd whip up a 'jus', but I personally find Bisto Instant gravy granules have a certain *je ne sais quoi* and a bottle of Co-op dressing tossed over the salad, does the trick. I'm so bored with preparing meals nowadays; after what feels like centuries of cooking for a family of five and now just the two of us, the everyday necessity to eat is just a chore and a bore. If I lived on my own, I'd have either an omelette or a salad every meal time, but Peter likes his meat and two veg and I still feel it's my job to do it. I'm not sure why … he's quite capable of cooking a meal when he sets his mind to it.

Our generation of husbands like to pretend that even though they've held down difficult jobs, bought houses and sorted out finances, putting a meal together is completely beyond them. The generation before couldn't even make a cup of tea, so I suppose there's been *some* progress, but compared to the modern husband who, not only holds down a difficult job, buys houses and sorts finances, but *also* manages to change nappies, cook, clean and get up in the night for crying babies, my generation of husband is a beginner. Peter *did* change the odd nappy, to be fair and he *did* get up in the night, but cooking has always been something for me to do. He does *sometimes* cobble a meal together and I'm meant to be eternally grateful and complimentary, as if he's done something quite extraordinary, which he has, I suppose.

"Wow, this bacon and egg is done to perfection," I'll say, whereas, deep down, I really want to say, *I've done this every day for the past million years. What's the big deal?* One thing that really gets on my wick is when the meal is ready, piping hot, on the plate, on the table and he doesn't even bother to show up. Tonight, I've yelled through the door and just got a desultory 'OK' and no actual movement.

"Peter, it's getting cold," I shout again, sitting down huffily in front of mine.

Still nothing. I start drumming my fingers on the table, imagining a scene in which I march in there and actually tip the lot on his lap.

"Peter! I'm going to start," I say and start stabbing the steak with venom.

He saunters in, "Sorry, just had to watch the end of the ..." Here, you can fill in the gap ... it could be cricket, golf, rugby, Grand Prix, snooker – take your pick.

He sits down and says, "Any mustard?" as if it's going to magically exit the cupboard and wing its way over to him.

"Glad you could join me," I say. "I don't like to interrupt your busy schedule with a beautifully cooked sirloin steak."

"Don't be like that ... it was such a tight finish ... Hamilton just nailed it, in the final lap."

"I'm so pleased for him," I say, automatically getting up and fetching the mustard. We both tuck into our meal, me sawing through the not-so-tender steak, wishing I'd foregone the meat completely. I rarely eat it these days; when I do, I find myself thinking about the poor animal I'm cutting through. It's disgusting, if you really start thinking about it. I wonder how many people would be prepared to: a) kill an animal b) get the fur off c) gut it? It's all so divorced from the animal, in its air-tight, plastic wrapping these days, that it's hard for people to see it for what it is. I know I couldn't do any of the above. In fact, I think I might be a secret Buddhist; this morning, I was washing out various dead insects from the bottom of the bath (I tend to shower these days) and a small spider, who'd been asleep, made a bid for freedom and dry porcelain. I helped him up the bath and watched with real joy, as he scampered away to lead his life.

"I should be a vegetarian, Peter. I don't like eating meat any more."

"This is delicious ... I couldn't live without it. Salad's for rabbits and wimps."

"Vegetarian meals aren't all about salad. There are grains, pulses, beans ..."

"It's your choice, but I don't want to give up meat. I'm a hot-bloodied man," he laughs, smearing

English mustard all over the steak rather disgustingly. I wonder if he'd be quite so keen if he had to run through fields with a spear?

Without him realising it, I have made our diet less dependent on meat. We often have vegetable curries, bolognaise made with Quorn ... and salmon. He never complains; I think he's just grateful to be fed. When I look back to when the kids were young, in the eighties, our diet was so unhealthy: lots of red meat and chicken Kiev, whatever *that* was – pieces of dubious-looking chicken with some horrid sauce around it, covered in a hard breadcrumb parcel, is how best to describe it. Pizza, sausages ... and for dessert: Angel Delight or, the height of luxury, Viennetta ice cream. So much of what we take for granted now, just wasn't available then. Tangerines were so rare that we even put them in the kids' stockings at Christmas. Imagine if you did that now? You'd be laughed out of court.

"Well, I might give up red meat completely," I said, leaving half of the steak on the side of my plate. Mabel looked longingly at it and I whispered to her that she could have it later. Peter also looked longingly at it and whipped it off my plate, before I could say anything.

The meal didn't take very long; there were no in-depth discussions about politics ... and so we cleared the plates, loaded the dishwasher (don't get me started on *that* procedure) and went and slumped onto the sofa. I flicked on the TV and scrolled through the guide to see if there was anything worth watching.

"Shall we carry on with that thing on Netflix?" I ask.

"Yea, there's nothing on the main channels, is there?"

"There never is, these days."

Since the pandemic, we've been watching Netflix, Prime, Apple TV – you name it, we've subscribed to it. I remember before lockdown, people of our age didn't have these streaming options, but it changed when we were all stuck at home for two years and so much of the output on the terrestrial channels dried up. Binge-watching whole series became a thing that we did, along with everyone else: *Bridgerton, Schitt's Creek, This is Us, Virgin River, After Life, Emily in Paris, Ted Lasso, Succession* – you name it, we watched it. This list is certainly not comprehensive and are mostly *my* choices. Peter's choices involve sport and oh! ... sport. We tend to like vaguely the same dramas, which is good, as we spend an inordinate amount of time watching TV. They are things that are 'easy' to watch and don't involve too many brain cells. This time, however, we're watching something with a complicated plot and even the recap doesn't really help. We haven't watched it for at least a week and now, it's as if we've never watched it before in our lives.

"Who the hell *is* that? Is that the guy who got beaten up or is it the guy who married that blond girl?"

"God knows. And I can't even remember why he

got beaten up, in the first place. I can't remember anything. Which *country* are we even in?" I say, in desperation.

"Let's just watch it ..."

Peter gets irritated with me, if I keep asking questions, surprisingly.

Part of being old is we now have subtitles on. I started putting them on because we were watching a film with very naturalistic speech *and* an American drawl; we couldn't understand a word. I tell myself that the modern direction of television and films is to make it SO natural that it's difficult to hear, but I'm probably going deaf. I know when the kids come home they find it hilarious how loud we have the volume and find it annoying with the subtitles on, but if I don't have them on, I feel I might miss something vital ... like the words. I keep putting off going to the doctor to get an audiology appointment; I can't bear the thought of wearing a hearing aid.

Pardon?

We struggle through the drama and by the end of the episode, I've just about got to grips with who is who. It's not really my scene, to be honest; it involves violence, swearing and sex, but I often subject Peter to love stories, costume dramas and comedy, so I feel I should persevere with it. He's enjoying it, I can tell. He says he's already worked out what's going to happen, which doesn't surprise me; he often *does*, and annoyingly, he's usually right. Endings of things always disappoint him; they're either predictable, weak or pathetic. He could have written a much better *denouement*, apparently. *Convoluted bollocks* is often his TV critic's opinion.

"How many more episodes are there?" he asks.

"No idea ... hold on, I'll scroll to *Episodes and More*. So, it seems we're only on Episode 4 of 10 and we're only on Series One – there are three more series. Oh God, I'm not sure I can bear nearly forty more hours of this."

"I'm quite enjoying it now that I'm into it ... shall we watch another one now, so that we're really back into it again?"

I give in and anyway, Netflix has kindly already started the next episode for us. It recaps the episode we've just watched and I vaguely remember the plot that I've only just this second, stopped watching. Sometimes, I think these TV execs deliberately complicate a story with flashbacks and flash-forwards and dream sequences. A straightforward story told chronologically would be preferable, but that's just not the way it's done these days ... too easy.

"Are we in the past or have we moved eleven years on?" I ask, innocently.

"Just watch it, *for God's sake* and you'll find out."

Peter's tolerance for my constant questions is running thin. "We're in the past, you can see how young he looks, can't you?"

Can I? He looks the same to me, but with a different hair style.

"Oh ..." I mutter, reaching for my phone. I know if I don't concentrate I'll have no chance of following this complicated plot, but with half an ear on the dialogue, I scroll blank-eyed through Facebook. I flit through posts of people showing off. *Wonderful weekend in Paris with this lot!* captioning a photo of people grinning in front of the Eiffel Tower. Then to ads for teeth whitening products that will probably strip your teeth of all enamel and onto clothes that look good value, until you order them and discover they're coming from China, via Timbuktu. Then, to companies telling me I *must* download their app *now,* so that I can manipulate my photos and make myself look twenty years younger. I always wish there was something in real life that could do that. Botox and lip fillers are the answer, maybe, if you want to end up looking not only like a freak, but an expressionless zombie who has been kicked in the mouth.

I pass numerous dog charity posts. I made the mistake of 'liking' lots of rescue dog charities and I'm constantly inundated with sad, homeless dogs staring into my soul. I genuinely want to rescue every single one I see; the ones in cages abroad somewhere, really get to me, but it seems daft to bring yet more dogs into the country, when all our charities are full up with our own poor, neglected mutts. I should 'unlike' them all, so that I don't have to upset myself every day, but for some reason, I can't. Mabel feels I should keep torturing myself, so that I appreciate her even more.

I flit over to Instagram; I started an account years ago, before anyone else had even heard of it. I liked the filters and the simplicity of it. I persevere with it today, still posting my photos, but it's now basically a place for people to show off and advertise, like Facebook for younger people. I still love it for the photography but as I scroll tonight, I watch an ad for someone selling a thing you can clip to the side of your bed to put things in. Heard of a bedside table, anyone? Then there's an ad by an earnest chap telling me about a microphone I could use on my phone which will improve the sound of my videos; it blocks out the wind, apparently. Then an ad for a broom – *This will be the best broom you've ever bought in your house.* I've never had the opportunity to buy a broom *in my house,* ever. You'd think they could get their grammar right, wouldn't you?

Bored, I go to my 'stories' which are no different from the posts – except they thankfully disappear after 24 hours, never to be seen again, which in most cases, is a blessed release. People share the kind of things that might be interesting to their partner or family, but to a complete stranger, are banal in the extreme. Cue artistic videoing of a full case with the caption: *How am I going to fit everything in?* Why is this of any interest? I feel like shouting to the phone, *Take something out or shut the fuck up,* but maybe that wouldn't be the sanest thing to do. Or ... the next story ... *Wonderful catch-up with this one!* and a picture of two beaming faces. Good for you ... you've met up with a friend. Why do I need to know? Or ... the next one ... a nauseating quote about Life - *It takes time to heal, but it also takes courage.* Why are you telling me this? To show how brave you are, for having simply got up this morning?

I feel such an old cynic and you may be wondering why I bother with social media, if I hate it so much? Well, for the same reason everyone else does, I suppose. To see posts from real friends and family who've done something I'm *actually* interested in. Facebook and Instagram, now both the same company, have lost their original intentions and have sucked us all into this Metaverse of advertising, without us realising it's happened. People now *advertise* their own lives under the impression that complete strangers will be interested.

The groups dedicated to your local area should be useful but are often full of people moaning and whinging and being positively unpleasant about everyone and everything, in the neighbourhood. If I want some entertainment, I sometimes read the comments about cars or vandalism in the area – basically, all teenagers should be hung, drawn and quartered and all drivers should be either jailed, or their cars towed away. Reading the comments you'd think we live in the violent suburbs of New York, not a peaceful country town. And God forbid if you let fireworks off or have loud music playing on a summer's night after about 9 pm. The *'don't have any fun*' brigade comes out in force.

There is a section of both of the platforms I quite like – the reels. I enjoy watching cats and dogs doing ridiculous things; if I feel a bit down, they cheer me up. I'm simple like that. I also like people falling off things.

Peter is nodding off beside me; his head keeps banging backwards and then violently comes back up again. He opens his eyes … then closes them again. This is repeated until his head finally stays resting on the wall, his neck bent at a terrible angle. He begins to puff and blow loudly through loose lips, which serves to distract me from both social media and the unfolding drama on Netflix. I've *literally* now 'lost the plot' on the TV and as Peter appears to be asleep, I sneakily exit Netflix and scroll down the Guide to see if there's something moronic I can watch. Perfect, a repeat of Gogglebox. I know it's a repeat because they're watching *Strictly* from last year. The whole concept of Gogglebox is mindless in the extreme – watching other people, watch TV … but for some reason, it makes me laugh. The gay guys from Brighton have such great lines … the Asian family with their razor-sharp observations … the posh couple in Wiltshire, who sit on chairs that match their wallpaper and who call each other 'Nutty' and the wonderful woman and her gay friend who are in the caravan. She's a natural comic, but also cries at anything. The banter between them cracks me up. So you can see what Peter's up against, I'm not the most intellectual of TV watchers. I wake him when I belly laugh at something they've said.

"What's happened to …?"

"Well, you were asleep so I …"

"Oh … was I?"

"Yes, strangely you've been out for the count for half an hour. Shall we go up?"

"Yes, I'm off to my scratcher," he says. This is an Air Force expression and sounds rather unpleasant. It conjures up bed bugs and rough blankets. He heaves himself off the sofa, as if he's about ninety and shuffles off. I take Mabel out for her final pee. She resents this – she just wants to get into her bed, but she wanders out. She stands on the grass, looking around the garden, as if we've got all the time in the world.

"Come on, do a wee," I shout, crossly. She looks at me, squats at last and then trots back in, gets into her bed and waits patiently for me to give her three biscuits. I kiss her head and say *Sleep Well.* I turn off the lights and walk slowly upstairs, clutching my phone. Peter's already asleep. It never ceases to amaze me how quickly he can drop off. Two minutes max. I always say to him that men are simple creatures and have nothing in their heads that worry them and keep them awake. He counters, with women just worry about everything and interfere with everyone else's lives and that's why I can't sleep.

We're probably both right, in our own way.

I get into bed to read my back-lit Kindle in the dark. It's like a repeat of the Netflix thing; I can't remember anything about this book or even which book it is. That's the trouble with Kindles, you have to make an effort to see the title. I give up after a few minutes. The dialogue is totally lost on me.

I close it and lie in the dark, reflecting on my riveting day.

CHAPTER 3

"Love at first sight is easy to understand; it's when two people have been looking at each other for a lifetime that it becomes a miracle." —Sam Levenson

Us – Back In 1970

So, that was us in 'modern times'; a typical day in the life of Peter and Sarah.

Going back to 1970, how on earth did these two meet? These two old people whose existence now seems to revolve around eating cake, dog walking and shouting at random people on the phone.

Well … it was the unlikely combination of sport and fags.

It was the summer of 1970 and Peter was playing in a lot of tennis tournaments; not something you would necessarily associate with smoking … but anyway. He was a fantastic player, was highly competitive, fit and he loved the game. I was in my final year at school, doing my A levels, no doubt very diligently.

I had a very pretty friend with long, straight, brown hair, with a flawless, round face and big blue eyes. For some reason I now can't recall, she was at the same tennis club as Peter, one sunny afternoon. I don't think she was playing tennis, maybe she was just there to watch but ... the moment that sealed our fate was when Peter, in between sets, obviously trying it on, asked her for a light. In those days, smoking was sexy and asking for a light was a good chat-up line. I'm pretty sure he would have had a lighter on him, he never went anywhere without his packet of twenty B and H and a plastic lighter. His opening gambit obviously paid off and after much chatting up, he and his tennis partner managed to wangle an invitation back to her parents' place, which wasn't exactly around the corner. The tennis club was in Guildford and she lived in a village, quite a few miles away.

The second thing that sealed our fate to live a lifetime together was that they all rang *me*, '*for a laugh*' and I chatted innocently to them for quite a time, not knowing what fate had in store. The upshot of *this* was that we all arranged to meet at Guildford Bus Station. I know, the romance of it is slightly overwhelming. If this had been a film, it would have been somewhere a bit more salubrious: maybe on a wind-swept beach, a beautiful garden or on top of a picturesque hill, but this was real life and Guildford

Bus Station was the backdrop to our love story.

I don't have much memory of what we did. I suppose when you're seventeen, you don't have to *do* much, but hang out and be cool. So, maybe that's what we did. Anyway, it was the rather inauspicious beginning to our lifelong relationship. Little did we know then, that fifty years later, I would be looking back and remembering this meeting of teenagers at a bus stop, through the mists of time, wondering 'what if?'

I like to ponder on the randomness of life. How totally weird it was that we came together that day. If my friend had ignored Peter's request … or indeed had *not* had a light, I wonder who I would have met and where I would have ended up? Our three children wouldn't exist. Was I ready to meet the man of my dreams that day, or was it just happenstance? If you believe in Fate, then it was *meant to happen* – but I can't help feeling that there are so many people I *could* have met and simply just *didn't*. If you believe in only *one* soul mate, then it's quite a coincidence that we both happened to live in Surrey, isn't it? I know this seems a cold and unromantic conclusion and I'm not that kind of person; I'm an old romantic at heart and an emotional wreck on many occasions, but … it just seems too strange. Like *Sliding Doors*, if my friend had not gone there, or had gone to the loo when he wanted a light, maybe he would have asked another girl and I'd never have met him. Or maybe he would have just used his own lighter?

But … on with this tale of young love. My School Council dance was looming; it would be called a Prom these days, but it wasn't as sophisticated as it is now; it was just some music in the assembly hall at school. I'm not sure we were even allowed alcohol and I certainly didn't spend a fortune on a fancy dress and a chauffeur-driven car, like they do these days.

Much to my shame, I wasn't going out with anyone at the time and, rather than go without a partner, I followed my friend's advice. She'd said to me, "Why don't you ask Pete Knights?"

Were ever six words so prophetic? I hardly knew him, but, to be honest, I was desperate, so I asked him and he said *yes*. Looking back, I'm pretty sure the invitation to a girls' private school was the attraction, not *me*. I can remember fancying him and thinking he'd reject the invitation, but he didn't, thankfully.

The one, abiding memory of the evening that I can still visualise clearly, is before the dance even started. We were to meet at *The Jolly Farmer* pub on the river in Guildford (I don't think it even exists any more or if it does, it's under a different name). Peter was bringing an unknown friend along to partner a friend of mine … another loser, without a boyfriend. We all assembled in the pub garden on a balmy summer's evening, at the allotted time and the only person who didn't turn up, was Peter Knights. There was quite a large group of us and his friend, whom none of us had met before, duly turned up and managed to chat easily to his proposed partner, despite never having met her before. I was left wondering if I would, indeed, be the sad loner at the dance, when, twenty minutes late, Peter appeared.

I can still see him now ... running down the steps into the garden: long, wavy, blond, wet hair, dark green suit, no tie ... and plimsolls. We'd call them trainers now, but they were most definitely white sports shoes. A curious fashion choice – certainly somewhat eccentric. His fashion choices still, to this day, are strange: canvas summer shoes for walking on extremely muddy fields in the winter, as just a brief example.

"Sorry I'm late ... been playing cricket."

And so it began ... a lifetime of 'just-in-time' arrivals and sporting interference. If I'd known *then* the number of sports events that would loom into my life and the casual approach to time, maybe I'd have just spent the evening at the dance and then parted company forever with our plimsoll hero. But ... the dance was a success: I arrived with this good-looking, long-haired, skinny guy and no doubt got envious glances from my classmates and a lot of streetcred. He enjoyed himself: he fancied my young, very attractive English teacher and he and his friend spent most of the time ogling her from afar. I assume we danced, but I can't remember us doing so. My memory just doesn't give me many memories of the dance ... just the vision of him running down those steps, into my life. So, then I left school and we started going out; I was keen, but trying very hard to appear 'laid back' and *cool*.

One thing that we both remember is 'The Guildford Show Incident'.

He lived in Guildford and I lived in a tiny village in the Surrey hills. I said I was going to the Show and that I would call in to see him, 'if I had time.' I was, in fact, remarkably 'uncool' with boys in those days. As recently discovered diary entries revealed, I was positively boy-mad and pursued them relentlessly. It was relatively innocent in those days, though – there was a lot of snogging and phone calls but not much else; very different from how it would be today. We'd probably have had sex at the school dance now or at least, soon after it. But I remember trying my best not to be over-keen with Peter, which means I *must* have felt strongly about him from the beginning.

The Guildford Show Incident was a triumph. For me. I deliberately hadn't called in to see him and I can still remember his rather put-out phone call in the evening, saying that he'd waited in for me and why hadn't I come round? The feeling when I got off the phone was one of victory to me – a definite 'one point to me' in the 'cool' stakes. He, however, vehemently denies that is how it went, still to this day, but I know for once, I was the cool one and … it worked. His interest in me was piqued. Maybe he'd never had a girl play the cool card before; he was very popular with the ladies, I'm told.

Anyway, for whatever reason, we started going out

… and so it all started.

#

When you write a romance or a love story, you have to invent barriers and problems so that the couple can't get together immediately. A story without difficulties would be a boring read and over, in a couple of chapters. Romances always have happy endings though, so if I was writing this as a novel, Romance would definitely be the genre I'd choose. So … Life invented quite a lot of problems for us along the way, just to add spice to this 'boy meets girl' story.

We'd met, but when you're seventeen and nineteen, there are other things that get in the way, like: needing to earn money; the relentless pursuit of fun; academic studies; careers, friends and members of the opposite sex.

I'd pre-arranged to spend my summer down in Cornwall with my best friend. We were going to work in a fish and chip shop (the sophistication of my life, then) and surf, when we weren't working (a little more cool). We were to live as lodgers in some old woman's house and live the dream, for a few weeks. So, we carried on with our plans and I disappeared out of Peter's life, to become steeped in chip oil and the surfing dudes of Polzeath. The confidence of youth meant that we met loads of people down there and had the time of our lives. I have strong memories of long queues at the fish and chip shop (*More cod up my end, please, Bill*, being a joke that still resonates) but also every spare hour in the waves, going to bonfires on the beach, in the evenings and even surfing in the dark, with the waves crashing over me, unexpectedly, as I couldn't see them coming. (Surely a metaphor for love?) I also remember walking home, back to the lodgings on my own in the dark, up the hill to Trebetherick, something I'd have hated my children doing ... but I survived marauding serial killers and rapists and made it through the summer unscathed.

I also remember getting a letter from Peter, saying words to the effect, that he'd met a Danish girl and was going to Denmark. The wording in the letter was: O*wing to this meeting and subsequent meetings, I'm going to Denmark.* This really makes me laugh now, but at the time, I was upset. It has always made me think that he'd copied some sort of text book on how to piss your girlfriend off, because the wording was just not *him*. I *was* pretty devastated though, but ... I was having a good time and if that's how he felt, *well, bugger off, then.* It's all so long ago now. It's hard to know how we ever got over this particular little obstacle, but we *did* and we carried on down the road to our future together.

I had a very exciting gap year ... *not* travelling to Australia or backpacking my way through Thailand, but very sensibly (and boringly) spending a year at Guildford Tech, doing a secretarial course. God, I knew how to have fun. I'm not at all sure why Peter liked me. I was so earnest and sensible and he was the polar opposite, but as I've said before, we really were (and are) two very different characters. Anyway, I mock … but it was a good move in the end because during my uni holidays, I used to get well-paid jobs as a secretary, which helped finance my life. The course saved me from lots of bar-tending and waitressing and gave me opportunities that wouldn't have existed without it. I worked, for example, for an estate agent, an insurance company and a cookery school. I also got a glimpse of commuting to London, working for an agency who sent me off to places, at a moment's notice. As I ran full tilt up escalators to catch the train home, however, I think I decided then that this wasn't the life for me at all. Little did I know, however, that the career I eventually chose, indeed *felt* like I was trying to go *up* the *down* escalator.

I went off to Birmingham University in 1972, in my little, old VW Beetle. Peter stayed in Guildford, working on the dustcarts, a career choice his parents were thrilled about, as you can imagine, but that he enjoyed, as he could make quite a bit of money 'totting', (for the uninitiated, this meant selling off old sofas and other bits of crap that people chucked out). He'd started the 'carts' as a student job, but when he failed his second degree, he worked as a bin man, full-time while trying to work out what to do next. He applied for the Air Force and to a bank; the RAF offered him a job, first. Working as a dustman certainly showed he was prepared to get his hands dirty and work long hours; the Air Force must have been impressed. Maybe it showed them that he would be prepared to have a lot of shit thrown at him during his military career. He eventually joined the Air Force in 1973, actually taking a pay *cut* to become an Acting Flying Officer, which seems daft, but true.

The first time he came to visit me at university, having joined the RAF, I can remember being mortified; *not* because I'd met another boy and *not* because I was heavily into having fun and he was interrupting my independence or anything like that ... but because he'd had a '*short back and sides*' haircut. How superficial I was ... but hair was *very* important in the seventies. Every male our age had long hair; not in the sense of it flowing down the back long, but it covered the ears, it flopped, it was 'full'. When Peter walked into my room that day, all I could see were his ears. He's actually got small, discreet ears, which don't stick out, but they appeared to have grown and reddened since I'd seen him last and I was *so* embarrassed. It felt like he was the only boy in the *entire* university who had short hair. And that mattered, in my young eyes. Poor guy ... the fact that he'd made the effort to come and visit me and driven for an hour and a half, obviously just didn't register.

We carried on seeing each other throughout my time at university; he'd visit from all the different Air Force stations he was being sent to: Church Fenton, Finningley, Lynham and St Mawgan. He failed his pilot's training unfortunately and, looking back, I'm sure it didn't help that he was *always* coming to see me. I'm not sure how he coped with all the training he was having to do, followed by hours of driving, drinking and partying at uni at weekends. He says it was a good thing he failed, as he probably would have killed himself. We'll never know, but thankfully he survived hours of flying by other pilots, as he became a navigator.

I know I didn't appreciate the amount of driving he did at the time, but *now* I do. I've just watched the new Beckham Netflix documentary and their relationship reminded me of ours, minus the millions. David used to drive for four hours to spend an hour or so with Victoria and that's what it was like with us: every spare moment, Peter would get in the car and drive to see me. He was so familiar around the hall of residence I lived in, I think a lot of people *thought* he was one of the students, despite the military haircut. He came to Philosophy lectures with me, I remember; I was studying English Literature, but I did a three-year module on Philosophy. Peter showed much more understanding of the subject than me. The Mind/Brain Identity Hypothesis went right over my own brain, but we used to discuss it together, as students do. The only way I passed the exam was to waffle endlessly and bore the examiner into submission. Peter had the advantage of swanning into the lecture theatre purely to listen and then swan out again.

He eventually found his niche. He discovered he could navigate a plane with his eyes closed – well, not literally, but metaphorically. His amazing maths ability came to the fore and he could put it to practical use, instead of studying Advanced Mathematics at uni, which really didn't suit his personality. This was an alien world to me – they were taught to navigate using the stars, for heaven's sake. For someone like me, who's got *dyslexia of direction* (which I'm sure is a genuine condition) he seemed like a magician. I'm someone who turns the wrong way down the corridor in a hotel, when I come out of my room. I was having a relationship with someone who could, I remember, many years later, navigate his way across Sydney, Australia, just by looking up at the sun. Sydney is notoriously difficult to find your way around; we had no map or navigation system and I remember Peter saying things like, "It must be this way, as the sun's on my left." It was an absolute miracle. If I'd been in charge, we would have still been lost in the backstreets years later, never to be seen again.

#

The course of true love continued and it soon became accepted that we would get married. I wore a ring on my left hand, even though we weren't officially engaged and, to be honest, I can't remember him ever really 'officially 'asking me. He certainly wasn't the 'get down on one knee in a public place' sort of guy and I would have hated it, if he'd tried it. I do remember us buying an engagement ring, in Kidderminster, of all places. Two sapphires and a teeny-tiny diamond.

There then followed the most bizarre episode of our 'courtship' and a definite bloody big barrier in the road to married bliss. We were going to get married in the summer of 1975, the year I left university. I think I may have blanked this from my memory because, for the life of me, I can't remember my reasoning (or lack of it), but ... I chickened out of the wedding. Everything was organised: the venue was arranged, we'd even sent out the invites and the cake was made.

Total nightmare.

I *think* I wanted to stay on at uni to do a Phd. I was very into academic work and I felt 'rushed' into getting married. Why I couldn't have decided this earlier, I don't know; as I said, I can't recall. I know the whole RAF thing slightly terrified me, too. I was going to have to submit to the Air Force way of life and I really didn't want to. I'd had nothing to do with the military during my life and wondered whether I'd like it, or would fit in.

I'm amazed that even *this* didn't break us up. Poor Peter. He must have felt utterly humiliated by me suddenly saying *no* to 1975. I said I wanted another year and I would deign to marry him, in 1976. I think if it had been the other way around, I would have told him to get lost, but thankfully, he didn't.

Not only was that a stupid thing to do, to postpone the wedding, but I also made completely the wrong decision, to do a PGCE (post-graduate certificate of education) instead of a Phd that year. If ever someone was not suited to teaching, it was *me*. How different my life would have been if I'd never done that course. I still regret it to this day.

All I can say, in my defence, for all this heartbreak, is that I was still *so young*. When we did eventually tie the knot in 1976, I was only twenty-three. A mere baby. By today's standards, I was crazily young. People in their thirties nowadays are still leading lives that we were living as twenty year olds; people seem to be getting younger and younger – or is it that I'm just so old? But people are definitely getting married much later now; when you're twenty-three, you haven't got a *clue* really, have you? Unless you're one of those people who've always known they want to be a doctor or an actor, most people have *no* idea what they want to do with their lives at that age.

So, I look back and try to see my dithering in that light and give myself a bit of slack. In fact, I'm quite impressed with myself that I was able to come to such a drastic decision at all, despite the consequences. I got a lot of stick about it from a) Peter and b) my mother, but it can't have been an easy decision to make and knowing what I'm like now, when I can't even decide whether to buy black or blue jeans, it seems quite courageous.

So ... on 14th August, 1976, we got married and forty-seven years later we're still together.

Maybe I can forgive myself for that lost year?

CHAPTER 4

"We're friends, too. We love each other, but we actually like each other—and that's an important distinction there. Love is passion and all of that stuff, but actually liking somebody and enjoying someone's company is something slightly different, and it lasts longer. So you can have both, and I think that's important. Be married to your best friend." —Sting

Me, Mum And My Life Before Peter

This story is divided into two halves: me, before Peter and me, after Peter. So, how did I even get to be seventeen years old? The *me* before Peter seems like another person entirely. How did I evolve and become the young, innocent, *naive* person who met that handsome, skinny tennis player and ended up living with him for the rest of my life?

I was born on January 30th, 1953 in Chelmsford,

Essex – yes, I know, forever an Essex girl. There have been many jokes along those lines ... blond, stupid etc. Why have Essex girls been subjected to this for so long? Surely the *woke* police has finally put a stop to it now?

Anyway, I don't remember living in Essex. My earliest memory is being in a cot in our house in Surrey, in the small, beautiful village of Holmbury St Mary, Surrey. I don't *think* it's a false memory; I remember the bars and the feeling that I was stuck in there and unable to climb out. I was in a little bedroom, known as the *office*. All I know is that I was crying and nobody came. It's a sad memory when I think about it, but normal in those days to leave a child crying. I probably cried myself to sleep in the end.

My father took a lot of photographs and cine films when we were young and so memories of my childhood may come from seeing these. (I have recently transferred those ancient films onto USB sticks). There I am: in the garden; on beaches in Cornwall; on a bike in the road outside our house and on ponies, often with my older sister, Deborah, but also with other, forgotten children. The adults – aunts, uncles, friends – all dressed in what looks like their Sunday best, but I think that's how people dressed in those days. None of this casual jean-wearing, that our generation has.

The films start off in black and white and then turn into colour; a world away from the slick iPhone videos we can all produce so easily now. There's no sound, just some rather awful background music that was added years later, but these moving pictures of me, at the age of two or three and older, evoke such a weird feeling. I'm round, very blond ... my clothes are often boyish ...yes, that really is *me* but a *me* that's forgotten. Still photographs are great, but seeing yourself moving, smiling and laughing, really brings it home how long ago it was.

Did I have a happy childhood?

If you look at these nostalgic, grainy films, it seems I did. A life in the country, with dogs and ponies and holidays by the sea. But ... when I look back now, with the benefit of hindsight and time, I realise that perhaps it wasn't as straightforward as it appeared.

This certainly isn't one of those memoirs about a terrible childhood, but mine had its problems. Mum was a marvellous mother and any happy memories are as a result of *her*; there were seemingly endless picnics – we *actually* ate cucumber sandwiches, sitting on a rug on grass, or sand. There was lots of swimming in the sea and in pools, always with Mum close at hand. We owned ponies, even though Mum had no prior knowledge or experience of horses and certainly had never ridden one. She managed to find fields that we could put them in, at a school for mentally-handicapped children (as we called them then) where she worked; she must have negotiated with the headmaster for us to put our ponies in their fields for free, I think, as we didn't have much money. She would constantly take us there to feed and look after them. One strong memory is of us picking hundreds of daffodils from those same fields and bringing them home, in buckets. We once counted fifty different varieties of narcissi and daffodils. You don't appreciate what your mother does for you when you're a child, but now I can see how amazing she was, working all the time and always making sure we had fun.

My father, however, was a totally different story. I don't remember him taking part in anything fun at all. He was a presence in the house, a moody presence, that we all had to endure. Now, he would definitely have 'mental health issues' and probably be diagnosed as 'depressed' in the real sense of the word, or even as bi-polar. Whatever was wrong with him, his moods inflicted themselves on all of us, *all* the time. He would sometimes not speak for weeks and I remember him sitting in the car for hours, while we were on the beach.

Mum was so good at parenting that she more than made up for his total lack of empathy and care. I was unaware that this situation affected me until relatively recently; it was only when I suddenly realised that I'd written a whole trilogy about what makes a real father (I didn't see it at the time I was writing it) that I understood how the absence of a real father *had* probably affected me hugely.

I say 'absence' but he was at home until I was thirteen, even if he wasn't partaking in family life.

Thankfully, he finally left us and the house was suddenly a place with no tension. He might as well have been physically absent before then, though. I remember finding Mum in bed in tears one morning and her telling me that he'd gone. I innocently said to her, "Why are you crying? It's a relief that he's gone, isn't it?" and she replied, "You'll understand when you're older." To me, the fact that he'd gone meant our house could be 'normal 'but of course, that was just a child's view and I now fully understand why Mum was crying. She was left with two girls and in those days, it wasn't easy for a woman on her own and however much they disliked each other, I suppose the reality of her situation was harsh.

When he was there, I remember sitting at the top of the stairs at night, listening to them argue ... and hating it. I don't know whether this was related, but there was a period when I kept climbing out of my bedroom window and crawling along the ledge to my sister's window. I was always disturbing her, going into her room in the normal way, so I was locked in so that I couldn't go to her room. To get around this problem, I got out of the window instead. This was a dangerous thing to do – we weren't in a bungalow and my bedroom and my sister's was on the first floor. I have no idea what was going through my head at the time or what I was trying to achieve, but that doesn't seem like a 'normal' thing to do as a child. It was always laughed about, as if it was a funny, family story to tell, but to me now, it seems like a plea for help, in some way. I know my mother had to bribe me to stop doing it, by saying I wouldn't be allowed to have my new school uniform and that I'd be the only one at the school without one, if I carried on. She told me afterwards that she'd never have carried out the threat and indeed had the uniform secreted at home, but what a disturbed little thing I must have been. Very sad.

My father smacked me so hard for something once that I had bruises all over my bottom and legs. I don't know what I'd done, but again, that isn't a good memory to have, is it? Smacking was commonplace then but to be covered in bruises isn't right.

So, that's why I was so relieved when he finally left. My sister and I didn't hear *anything* from him for over ten years, (how can a father totally ignore their children for TEN years?) by which time, I'd moved on into early adulthood, had met Peter and didn't really *want* to see him. We did have a couple of encounters with him, but when he eventually died in a care home, he didn't want us to be informed, apparently. A solicitor, however, rang to tell us he'd died (he thought we had the right to know) and we did, in fact, go to his funeral down in Cornwall, but the care home he was in, didn't even know we existed; he'd never mentioned us. How strange is that? I can remember feeling guilty because I couldn't cry and had no emotion at all. He was nothing to me.

I really wish I'd had the experience of good father. When I see my son-in-law with his children, I feel sorry for my younger self and I can see how very difficult it must have been for my mother. What a strong woman she was and how cruel life was that she eventually got Parkinson's Disease. I'd just started university in 1972; I spoke to my mother most days and one day she told me that she'd been to the doctors because she was 'finding it difficult to write'. She said 'don't worry, it's nothing important', but it turned out to be the beginning of Parkinson's Disease. She was only in her fifties when she got it and in the end, it was the thing that killed her – her body was so weak and unable to function, that it just gave up. She tried so hard for so many years to carry on, but even with a lot of medication, the disease took hold. Most people associate Parkinson's with the shakes, but she had the type that doesn't make you shake and leaves you unable to move. Her muscles were rigid and she often had staring eyes – she would get stuck in doorways, simply unable to go through them.

At first, when she went to be diagnosed, she was put in a mental hospital, as they thought she had some form of mental illness but eventually they realised she had Parkinson's. She was put on a regime of pills which worked well for quite a few years, but after a while, they had to be re-adjusted and it was difficult to get the balance right. She would sometimes have too many or sometimes too few and the effects of this would be devastating. Inevitably, she became obsessed with her pills, almost like an addict, who thinks the next fix will solve everything.

I remember one occasion when she'd been given too many of these pills and she was hallucinating. Mum always had a bit of a *thing* about the IRA (it was at the time when there was constant news coverage of bombings) and she thought all the doctors and nurses were members of the IRA and that bombs were under her bed in the hospital ward. Again, it sounds like a funny story, but actually it was very frightening at the time, for both her and us.

Before she got really ill, she did meet Peter. The first time they met, the thing I remember her saying was, "That boy has lovely hair". That always made us laugh. He did, in fact, have lovely hair, before it was all chopped off. It was before he joined the Air Force and his hair was long, wavy and every girl's dream. They eventually got to know each other and got on well and Peter was always very supportive to me (and her), as she got more and more disabled. We even seriously considered having her to live with us, but it was impossible in the end – she needed twenty-four hour care.

Mum ended up first in warden-assisted housing, then went into an old people's home and then inevitably, into a nursing home. These were all at least an hour from where we were living and I have strong memories of going to see her with three young children in tow, trying to take her out in her wheelchair for a walk. Mum was quite a big lady, not fat, but tall and big-boned, so the chair was heavy to push and trying to negotiate pavements and keep the kids away from the traffic, was a stressful experience. The alternative was to stay in the confines of her room, which wasn't right for any of us.

I do, however, remember taking her jelly babies every time I went to see her. How she loved sweets – but the reality of her life was dreadful. Her mind was still active, so she was fully aware of her fate. At least with dementia, you're unaware of the complete chaos you're causing. She wasn't a great TV watcher; I always feel in similar circumstances, I would be glued to the telly, but she listened to the radio and read.

What a way to end your days, stuck in an institution, with strangers. I remember her laughing and saying once, 'If I get too bad, just shoot me' and quite frankly, it would have been kinder. They shoot horses, don't they?

It was a shame that her illness prevented her from being a normal granny. I'm sure she would've taken them for long walks, swimming and for great picnics, but it wasn't to be.

I certainly put a lot down to my mother for my love of music, the countryside and animals. We had numerous pets when I was growing up: a ginger cat called Pepsi, two Boxers called Honey and Kim, hamsters called Mustard Seed and Vasco da Gama (he was always escaping) a rabbit called Fluffy and of course, the ponies. Mum used to love musicals and when she could, she'd take us to the theatre. We'd sometimes go to the Chichester Festival Theatre and see productions like *Half a Sixpence* and *Oklahoma*. She'd sing the songs in the car all the way home, and even now, when I hear songs from the musicals, I think of her.

#

One incident that has affected my life, even now, happened to me when I was ten. I was at a junior school run by a convent. I can still see the nuns in their wimples and robes; on the whole, they were kind.

The school was quite a long way away and I made friends with a girl who lived near it. The school had an open-air swimming pool and we were allowed to go to it in the summer holiday; I have a cine film of me there, at some gala, so I can 'see' it clearly.

I went to stay with my friend, Gillian, one day in the summer holidays and her mum dropped us off to swim. They lived near enough for us to be able to walk home, something I don't think you'd do now with ten year old girls, as the walk involved walking through woods and fields, not along pavements.

After our swim, we set off back to her place and in the woods, we started climbing trees, as any normal ten year old would. We noticed a lone man watching us, but in our innocence, we carried on. After a while, we climbed down and made our way through the wood to a field … and he followed us. I can remember what happened next, as if it only happened yesterday. Gillian was climbing over a stile and he grabbed her from behind. He threw her to the ground and she landed on some stones that later we found had injured her back. He got on top of her and all this happened without him saying *one* thing ... or making any sounds.

She was screaming and kicking and I was pulling her legs, trying to get her away from him. I don't know how long this lasted, that part of it is just a blur now, but I think he must have realised he had taken on more than he could deal with and just as suddenly as he'd got on top of her, he stood up and walked away.

When I think about this now, it was in broad daylight, in open countryside – anyone could have walked that way. He must have silently weighed up the pros and cons of the situation and decided it wasn't worth the risk with *two* little girls, both screaming and shouting. We ran home to her place and told her parents, who rang the police and we spent the rest of the day in a police car, looking for him. We also had to look through a book of mugshots of likely candidates, but we never saw him again.

Even though I wasn't the one he attacked, it was one of the most frightening experiences any child can go through and to this day, I don't like walking alone through woods. I wonder, if he's still alive, whether he ever thinks of those two little girls he traumatised? I doubt it. I'm just hoping he eventually got caught.

An incident like that can definitely affect you and not just in ways that make you cautious where you walk. I think it's made me generally a more anxious, nervous person than I would have been. When I'm alone in the house, I always make sure I'm *locked in,* even in daytime. I think I'm hyper-alert to danger; I try to 'look ahead' and anticipate things happening, which can be wearing for everyone else. I call it 'looking ahead' but my family sometimes call me pessimistic or negative … but I'm pretty sure it stems from this incident.

#

It's strange how incidents from your family's past can affect you, even though you weren't even born. When my sister was a baby, my parents' house burned down. This has been in our family history and has always been a part of mine, too. The fire started in my sister's nursery; no one was killed or hurt even, but my parents' entire house and belongings were destroyed. When I think about it, this can't have been a good start to any marriage and maybe laid the foundations for their unhappy life together. The house that was burned down was in Essex; my parents then moved to Holmbury St Mary, in the Surrey Hills. I don't know why, but presumably for my father's job. It was a beautiful village, with a church, a couple of pubs and about three shops and we lived at the end of a no-through road, leading off the village green. Where the road came to an end was the village hall and then, just miles of wonderful countryside leading up Holmbury Hill, which had magnificent views at the top. The hill was covered in bracken and pines, the soil was brown and sandy.

The next incident of fire happened when I was about three years old. I can't, in all honesty, remember it that clearly, but I can still *see* the skies filled with black smoke and the smell, permeating the air. You see, the whole of Holmbury Hill caught fire. Our house had pine trees behind, in front – all around us, in fact and I'm not sure if this is a false memory or not, but I can see what I was told were fifty foot flames engulfing the trees opposite our house. It was all on the TV and on the front of the Daily Mail (I have a copy); something like thirty fire engines arrived to fight the fire and all the villagers were out, beating the flames all night. A fire-break track was made behind our house to stop the fire, but our house bricks were burning hot to the touch. This house, too, could so easily have gone up in flames. But thankfully it didn't. The fire was eventually put out, but the hill took years to recover. I remember black skeletons of trees marching across the landscape for many years following and the long-lingering stench of burning.

My parents had to beat the flames, like all the other villagers. My God, they must have thought, *not again*. I can't imagine what they must have gone through.

So, these two incidents also entered my psyche – the fear of fire has crept into my mind and sat there, looking for possible outlets.

Whenever I leave the house, if it's me who has to do the last minute checks that everything's 'off', it takes me a while. I go back again and again to check.

My fixation has focussed itself on the iron, for some reason. Even though I don't iron any more (I went on strike about five years ago and now just *fold* things carefully) I still have to 'check the iron is off' when, in reality, I know I haven't used it for months and Peter hardly ever uses it. A mild form of OCD, I think. I've even been known to take a picture of said iron, unplugged, so that I can refer to it when, inevitably, I say to Peter on the motorway:

"I *did* turn off the iron, didn't I?"

He'll say, "Yes, of course you bloody did."

And I'll look at my phone, still unconvinced.

Life can be a bit cruel sometimes – making your mind play tricks on you and sending you momentarily, a bit bonkers.

#

As mentioned before, I went to a posh secondary school. I'm not at all sure how my parents afforded it, to be honest – maybe they weren't so expensive in those days?

One of my father's many job changes involved a foray into working abroad. He was very 'into' electronics – he could make his own radios (in pencil boxes and match boxes, I remember – very impressive) and I know he had a job to do with equipment that tested people's hearing. I remember playing with this when I was a child. It echoed your speech back into headphones and if you weren't genuinely deaf, you just couldn't speak. It was fun, but pretty useless looking back, as it didn't tell you anything about the level of deafness. My point here is that my father was always swopping jobs – my mum used to say he fell out with his bosses all the time, which I can well imagine. He'd have fitted in with today's penchant for moving jobs constantly, but in those days of '*a job for life*', he was unusual.

So, he suddenly announced that he'd got a job in Denmark – Copenhagen, to be precise. I'm sure my mother wouldn't have wanted to go but she *did* go and my sister and I were made to go to boarding school. I can't recall what the job was now, but it lasted two years, before he fell out with someone … and we all came home again.

The experience of going somewhere new was totally ruined for me, because I hated boarding. I was so unutterably miserable all the time, it was awful. I was homesick – a illustrative word, when you think about it. I was 'sick' because I wasn't at home. I missed my mum so much and I'm sure I made it extremely difficult for her at the beginning of every term; I remember sobbing uncontrollably every time I had to go back. She wrote me loads of letters, but I remember just feeling so sad *all the time*.

It was a 'high church' school which meant we spent our life in chapel and even now, when I hear church music, I can feel the sadness that used to dominate my life back then. It was crazy – on Sundays, we often went to chapel three times – an hour's communion before breakfast, evensong and sometimes, 'congy practice' too. This was when the congregation had to practise singing. I remember feeling so hungry in that morning service, I often felt faint.

I suppose it was a way of keeping us occupied at weekends – there wasn't much else going on. Boarding schools are now often more like hotels with five star food, incredible sporting facilities and a lot of freedom for the pupils. Then, I felt as if I'd been locked up in a penitentiary. We had four exeats a term where we were allowed out, but as my parents were abroad, it meant going to people's houses I didn't really want to go to.

We were sometimes allowed out to the local village on a Saturday, but this involved walking in a crocodile, with a teacher at the head. We were allowed to go into the local shop and I remember buying sweets and then binge-eating them. We weren't allowed to make phone calls, either – nowadays, kids can Whatsapp their parents all the time, I'm sure. What a difference that would have made to me.

It was quite exciting when my sister and I got on a North Sea ferry to Denmark at the end of term, I suppose, but I would have much preferred to be at home. I remember being on one of those ferries once when even the crew was being sick, due to the horrendous crossing. I've never been partial to ferries since.

I haven't got very many memories of my time in

Denmark. I had a crush on one of my dad's boss's sons – maybe this was the emergence of being aware of the opposite sex? I remember finding Danish houses very hot compared to English ones; we were amazed the way Danish people would strip off their warm clothes when they went inside. I also remember the cleanliness of everywhere compared to England: pristine pavements even in the heart of Copenhagen. I liked the open sandwiches they ate, but not the pickled herring.

One of the most terrifying experiences I had was at Tivoli Gardens – we went on a 'ride' which involved going into a circular room and it beginning to spin. It spun faster and faster until the people opposite us, looked as if they were above us. We stuck to the walls with centrifugal force and the floor was then taken away, so we were 'suspended' by nothing. As the spinning slowed, we gradually slid down and down. I can honestly say I was petrified. I wonder if that ride still exists today? Do some people think that's entertaining?

When my father eventually decided he didn't like this job, we all came back home. I, of course, desperately wanted to become a day girl immediately, but my mum was reluctant as it would involve me in a long journey there and back each day. I didn't care, I just wanted to stop boarding, at any cost. I eventually won the argument. Mum had to drive me to a bus stop and after that bus journey, I had to make a connection with another bus. I often missed my connection, but it was worth it. I was at last home, where I wanted to be.

When my father eventually left, he refused to continue paying the school fees. Mum went to talk to the Head and the upshot was, I was allowed to stay on at the school with a bursary. It would have been very disruptive to change schools at the time and I was grateful I could stay.

By then, I was having a ball as a day girl; boys had definitely raised their ugly heads and my friends and I were constantly out socialising – or more accurately, hanging around.

And then … I met Peter.

#

So, that was me, before I met Peter. There I was, innocently meandering along my single path and then, bang, I bump into my future husband.

When my friend said, *shall we meet at Guildford bus station*, should I have run for the hills? Might I have met someone else the very next day, or would I have had to wait for years before meeting another Mr Right?

Life is random, life is mysterious, life is unknown.

CHAPTER 5

"Marriage is a mosaic you build with your spouse. Millions of tiny moments that create your love story." —Jennifer Smith

My 'So-Called' Teaching Career 1978 – 1991, With Intervals

Why on earth did I think I wanted to be a teacher? I'm so wholly unsuitable. To be a teacher, you've got to be outgoing, confident, extrovert, to name but a few traits and I'm just about the polar opposite.

Even now, after all these years of living, you'd think I'd have got used to being *me*, but I haven't. I kind of assume people won't like me, which is limiting (and as a teacher, it's probably true of most of your pupils). It makes joining things, being part of things, hard; a constant voice in my head says things that I imagine other people are saying about me: *She thinks she's posh ... she's boring ... she's huge.* Do they say these things?

I don't know, but I suspect not. People have got their own problems to worry about and frankly, I'm just not *that* interesting. It doesn't stop me imagining them saying them, though.

I blame a student at university all those years ago for making me have a *thing* about being posh. He made some passing comment about my southern accent and it's stayed with me, ever since. I never really even knew I had a 'posh' accent until then. I'd lived 'down south' in Surrey, gone to a girls' private school, where everyone spoke the same way and I naively thought I was like everyone else. Once I got to Birmingham University, I had a rude awakening. People had all sorts of different ways of speaking and it seemed to define you. I can remember feeling mortified that I was the 'posh' one, but I was stuck with my voice and accent and there was nothing I could do about it. It wasn't in my nature to change my accent and I didn't have the ability to, anyway.

The same thing happened with my body image. Someone said once that I had child-bearing hips, as a *joke*. They thought it was hilarious, but I've had that comment ringing in my ears, ever since. There's something really *off* about the phrase. Not only does it make you sound like a baby-breeding machine, but it also totally defines your shape; you can't shave inches off your actual bones. I say it was *one* person who said it but, in fact, it's a phrase that's followed me around and *several* people have used it – always thinking they're being funny. People say: *Sticks and stones may break my bones, but words shall never hurt me* but boy, is that *not* true. Note to self – be careful what you say to people.

I try to ignore the self-doubt much of the time, but it's hard when you look in the mirror and see someone the size of Giant Haystacks staring back at you. Or when you hear your voice, recorded for some reason and you sound slightly posher than the Queen. Recently, I was looking back at an old video Peter took when we first moved to Cyprus and it honestly sounded as if Princess Diana was talking.

That modern expression, *it is what it is*, should apply, but it doesn't. You can live for seventy years and still not be comfortable in your own skin.

I wish I had Peter's confidence; he doesn't give a damn what other people think of him. He has no regard for other people's opinions and, in fact, according to him, most people's opinions are just plain wrong, anyway. He doesn't care that he's now Extra Large in most men's shirt sizes; in fact, he thinks it's funny and just eats more cake.

"What's the point of being miserable for ninety years? I'd rather die happy," he says, tucking into yet another slice of coffee and walnut.

He has a point.

When we first met, he was as skinny as a marathon runner; he did indeed run a bit, although the furthest he ran was a half-marathon, but that's further than

I've ever run in my entire life. He was so thin, he had *to run around in the shower to get wet* apparently, but I think that was probably an exaggeration.

I love the image that it conjures up, though.

#

So, someone with little self-esteem or confidence seems like an ideal person for doing a spot of writing – a nice, introverted activity where you don't have to communicate with anyone, except yourself. Unfortunately, it took me about sixty years to realise this. I really am well-suited to a rather insular, silent way of life, where I can pretend to be someone I'm not.

I can't remember doing creative writing at school; it was all too worthy and academic in those days. I did English 'A' level but that didn't involve any actual *creative* writing; it was all about regurgitating large chunks of books and plays and stringing it all together, to answer a question. All done from memory too. Not all this *taking the book into the exam* nonsense.

Then, onto uni to study English *again*. I'm not sure what I was thinking, looking back. How useful can English to this level *really* be?

Teaching it became the inevitable path I trod, which was definitely the *wrong* one, for me. Not *once* in these five years of 'A 'levels and a degree did I ever produce anything creative, something that had crawled out of my *own* brain. I was quite good, it turned out, at talking about other people's work and learning by rote. I'm not sure this was any good for anybody, but it kept me occupied for a few years

So this desire to write my own words crept up on me, slowly, slowly. Once I'd realised that teaching children was about the worst decision I'd ever made, I then gave birth to three of my own and I think that's when the creative spark was lit. I've since found lots of little pieces of writing I did at the time of being a busy mother; I think I was trying to make sense of the experience, but it wasn't until much later in life that I actually did something about it.

I can't get over how *clever* I was at uni. This is rather an indulgent thing to say, I know, but I still have all my files and notes and I feel like the person I was *then* had a bigger brain than my present self. This is probably true – I'm sure my brain has shrunk, while the rest of my body has increased in size. The intelligent handwritten notes I put in the margins of books are incomprehensible to me now and not just because they were scribbled, but because they showed an intellect that's now extinct. I had nine three-hour final exams, only *one* of which covered *all* of Shakespeare's plays. Another exam was entitled American Literature; a few books to remember there, then. I'd taken Philosophy as a subsidiary subject, as mentioned before and also had a three-hour paper on that to complete. I don't even understand the subject now, never mind being able to write about it for three hours. I remember one guy who only wrote for half of the three hours and then confidently put down his pen and walked out of the exam room. He got a first. I wrote furiously for three hours and got a 2:2.

To cap it all, I developed a problem with my neck. When I spent hours writing, it set off a nerve pain down my right arm (I write with my left), so I had to take all nine exams in the medical centre, while under the influence of strong pain killers. That's about as exciting as my life on drugs ever was.

Then, as mentioned earlier, I didn't do a Phd on some obscure literary subject which would have taken me three years but would have suited my personality more; I took the stupid decision to do a postgraduate year of learning how to teach English to bored teenagers, which mainly dealt with the theory of teaching, the history of education and other useful topics which were incredibly useful in the classroom. *NOT.*

I did two teaching practices during the year-long course. One was at the roughest school in Birmingham. When the list went up of where we were all being sent, I remember the sighs of relief when people realised it wasn't *them* who was going there and then the laughs, when they realised it was *me* who'd drawn the short straw. My experience there was like a living nightmare. This sounds like an exaggeration but ... I'll explain.

It was at the time of race riots around the country. A man in Handsworth had put up a sign in his window to rent out a room and had put NO BLACKS.

(It doesn't even feel *possible* now, but that sort of thing was common in the seventies.) This led to a riot, which I encountered when I innocently took my mum to see the school I was teaching in. I'd explained to her how awful it was and wanted to show her my place of torture. It was a Saturday, she'd come up for the weekend and we thought we'd just do a drive-by. As if to demonstrate the problem I was having, as we approached the school, we were surrounded by an angry mob of black people, who banged on the top of the car and we only just managed to extricate ourselves. The riot was on the TV news later.

"Well, it won't get any worse than that," Mum said, trying to be encouraging, but failing miserably. I'm not saying it *did* get worse than this, in terms of race relations, but this school certainly set a low bar and my teaching career never recovered. It was an inner-city comprehensive located near a prison. 98% of the pupils were coloured (as we called black people then). In walks innocent little me: English graduate, country girl, posh southern accent and ... white. I stood out like ... a white girl in a black school, but I was their teacher too and they hated me, or so I felt. I discovered that I'd been given all the unteachable classes, that no one else wanted. One of the books I was asked to teach to a mixed class of fourteen year olds, some of whom were taller than me, was *Black Beauty* – you couldn't make it up, could you? A sweet little story about a nice white girl and her pony. To inner-city black kids of both sexes. You can imagine how easy *that* was. I had to hand out the book, paper and pens at the beginning of every lesson and get them back in again, at the end. A forty minute lesson was taken up with that, mainly.

The only part of the day I enjoyed was the assemblies. It sounds very clichéd, but we sang some great Afro-Caribbean songs with rhythm and fun; so much better than dour, Church of England hymns which I was used to.

Peter often visited me from wherever he was during that year. During this teaching practice, he came to collect me one afternoon and was amazed at the fights going on around the car and the Head, standing by, not doing anything to stop them. Like my mother, he tried to put a positive spin on it, but nothing could dampen the effect it had on me. My non-existent confidence and self-esteem were at an all-time low. God knows why I continued down this path … money and school holidays, probably. Seriously, I think that *was* my reasoning: a career I absolutely loathed balanced against longer holidays than other jobs and quite good money.

What stupid decisions you make when you're young.

#

After the post-graduate teaching course year, we got married and before I knew what was happening, I was on the overnight train to Inverness.

Why? Because Peter was stationed at RAF Kinloss.

We'd had a gorgeous honeymoon in Tenerife, but the moment we got back, the reality of my situation hit me in the face. Not only had I had nothing to do with the Air Force before, but I'd never even been to Scotland. I assumed I'd be able to find a teaching job up there; I'd have all this spare time, so surely, now was the time to start this wondrous new career? Unfortunately, that wasn't to be. I'm not sure if it's the same now, but in those days, you had to have a Scottish teaching certificate to work in Scottish schools and so there I was, stuck up in the wilds of Scotland, with nothing to do.

I could have dedicated my life to being an officer's wife: flower arranging in the Mess and having coffee mornings with other wives ... but that somehow didn't appeal. I'd been put off this lifestyle by a 'wive's luncheon' I'd bravely gone to soon after I arrived and I'd been stuck at the bottom end of the table as I was, and I quote, 'Flying Officer Knights' wife'. I wasn't Sarah, oh no, I was an appendage. The conversation revolved around our husband's blossoming flying careers and I thought, 'Do you know what? This isn't for me ... at all'.

This was the seventies, and I'm sure it's very different for wives now, but I wasn't enjoying living in a married quarter, either. I didn't like the fact that we lived in houses depending on our rank, so my neighbours all had husbands with the same status, job, interests etc. I felt like a fish out of water, lonely, isolated and thoroughly miserable. Those of you who have read my book, 'Life Happens' may recognise this experience in Rachel; her dislike of military life is pretty much based on me.

I can remember taking cooking seriously for the first time in my life, just as a way of occupying myself and comfort eating. I think we both put on loads of weight. I also remember the kindness of the Station Commander whom I met at some social 'do'. He was actually interested in *me* and offered to help re the teaching problem. I never thought he'd remember me after the conversation at the do, but he later contacted me; unfortunately, there was nothing he could do. I think of him though, as he demonstrated great personal skills and communication, even with a mere wife.

The next thing we did was to buy a surrogate child, that is, a puppy. He was the first in the line of Labradors we've owned during our marriage. Toby came from true working stock and when we went to see him for the first time, he was in a cage with all his siblings, in a field, in the snow. When we left, to make our decision as to which one we wanted, it was *him* who stood on his back legs and begged us to take him with us. They say dogs choose *you* and that was definitely true of him. He was what is now called, *fox red* and I can *still* see him, standing there, paws against the chicken wire, surrounded by snow.

He proved to be a great companion for me. I have a picture of myself, wearing an Afghan coat (very seventies), with long blond hair, sitting on the floor, with Toby stretched out, lying upside down on my legs, in front of the RAF quarter's gas fire. He never used his breeding (to be a gun dog) and adapted to being a lap dog instead, with great alacrity. He was the most gorgeous dog but had his bad habits. Activities Toby enjoyed: chewing wires in our old Sunbeam Alpine, making it impossible to drive; stealing all the sausages from a pan on the cooker; weeing on our friends' Christmas tree when they'd offered to have him for a few days (I think he thought they'd kindly provided an inside tree for the purpose). He also stole and ate a bag of raw mince, including the plastic bag it was in, and a half-eaten chicken after an Easter lunch at my sisters'. The reason his following Labs in the line were all female was the constant lifting of his leg on things – the final straw being when he weed on the belongings of a man who had left them, in splendid isolation, on a completely empty beach.

Soon, however, I needed something more to do with myself than eating and walking and so, I applied for a job looking after horses, which had a cottage thrown in. This would kill two birds with one stone – it would get us off the camp *and* give me a job.

I got the job and it turned out that we would be living in the depths of the most beautiful landscape, near Forres. We could catch the scent of malt whiskey which was being made in the distillery down in the valley, from our cottage. The people I worked for were very definitely *posh* and it wasn't just the way they spoke, either. They had an enormous, stunning, turreted baronial hall, in many acres of land and we were to live in a cottage by the stables. I was to be the groom; I stupidly thought I would be friends with them, as they too were English. Unfortunately for me, I was quite definitely the *hired help* and treated as such.

They had two beautiful thoroughbreds and my job was to muck them out and saddle them up, ready for them to hop on. Nice life for them. I often had to exercise them myself and I had one terrifying ride when Wellington, the large bay, got spooked and bolted with me for what felt like hours. I was on my own and we were galloping down narrow paths with pine trees on either side, completely out of control. I bashed my foot on a tree trunk and to this day, I can still feel where I hit it. The only way I managed to stop him, was by standing up in the stirrups, leaning back and pulling so hard on the bit, I must have damaged his mouth. We were careering down a wider, sandy track by this time, which led home and it had a five-bar gate at the bottom. I pulled him up just before the gate, thank God. Maybe even *he* realised that vaulting it, would be a stupid move.

The worst thing about this job was the loneliness. Toby and I hardly ever saw *anyone* – the owners of the horses were unfriendly and Peter was away so much on Nimrods, I hardly ever saw *him* either. I'm not sure how I stuck it for two years, but I did.

The other terrible thing about the job was I lived 'on the job' and therefore was always available when I was officially *off duty*. I remember one particular day when the horses escaped and I spent my day off, trying to catch them.

It was also *effing* cold, all winter. I remember one day my nose felt odd; it was running ... but was turning into ice. That particular winter it was so cold that diesel was freezing and one day, I got a phone call to say that Peter was in hospital, as his car had hit ice and come off the road. He'd hit a tree and the top part of the tree had sheared off and landed, thankfully, *not* on the top of the canvas roof of our convertible MGB. Peter was fine, by the way, but that just added to the joys of living up there.

Another incident with the horses I remember with a certain amount of awe. The chestnut mare was 16.3 and for the uninitiated, that's a *big* horse. I can't for the life of me remember her name but she was a bit of a b-i-t-c-h in the stable. One day, she was tethered to a heavy, free-standing feeding manger by a rope, hitched to her halter. I was in the stable with her – she used to try to bite or kick if you did anything to her (maybe Peter's opinion of horses was indeed correct?) She jerked her head upwards and the feeding manger moved, which set her into a panic. Horses are very beautiful animals, but they haven't got a lot of common sense. The more she panicked the more the manger moved ... and the more she panicked. I was stuck in a stable with this enormous creature and it was a case of me trying to survive. I managed to grab her halter and with sheer brute strength that comes from somewhere in these sort of circumstances, I managed to pull her head down enough, to untie the knot that was attached to the manger and thus, release her. I can still feel the panic I myself felt in that small, dark stable with tons of horse flesh going absolutely berserk, at very close quarters to me.

I never did like that horse ... and liked her even less, after that.

#

Having at last moved south, we went to live in Lincolnshire, so that Peter could go to RAF Waddington. While he was off flying in his Hercules, I got a job, part-time, as a teacher; I thought I ought to, but didn't really have any desire to do it. I'd gone for a full-time job, but when I went for the interview, I found out that the other candidate was the Head of the English department's wife. *Great. So I'm not the number one candidate, am I?* But it turned out that she was going from part-time to full-time and I got offered *her* job. I suppose this was quite a nice way of being introduced into the rigours of teaching, on reflection, only doing part-time. It was a girls' grammar school and to be fair, it wasn't too bad, compared to my teaching practice. I had to teach history too and was only ever one page ahead of the children. I taught eleven and twelve year olds and they were quite sweet; it's only when they reach thirteen, they become horrible, fledgling teenagers. I lasted there a while, before being whisked away to our next posting.

My next foray into teaching was a few years later, when we were posted to RAF Lynham. A job came up at a very expensive and posh girls' private school – there seems to be a pattern emerging here, doesn't there? I was obviously trying to avoid schools that were remotely like my teaching practice school. This was also part-time and again, it was okay, I suppose, but I remember the feeling of dread I would get, as I got up each morning. The younger girls were nice, but I had to teach sixth-form girls too. They *had* to do English, even if they were doing science 'A' levels and I was the sucker chosen to teach them. They absolutely hated it and consequently felt honour-bound to make my life hell.

Those of you who are reading this because of my books about Cyprus, will know that we got posted to Cyprus in 1991. I was teaching at this posh school at the time and I can honestly say that I regarded Cyprus as an escape route out of teaching. If we hadn't gone, I probably would have stayed doing it forever and ended up a blithering wreck, so ... thank God, in this instance, for the RAF. There aren't many instances when the Air Force came to my rescue, but this was one of them. It whisked me away from hours of torture, stuck in a classroom with loads of children, teaching a subject I didn't want to teach, marking books I didn't want to mark, pretending I was someone I wasn't.

Instead, I landed on a Mediterranean island, with absolutely no prospect of being able to get a job at all; wives, in those days, weren't allowed to work in Cyprus.

What a blessed relief.

CHAPTER 6

"A successful marriage requires falling in love many times, always with the same person." — *Mignon McLaughlin*

1981 To 1986 – The Years Of Giving Birth

I've decided that this is my story and my children have their own stories to tell, so I'm going to leave them to write their own – but giving birth to them is part of *my* story … so here I go.

I always knew I wanted children; it was just simply part of my future that I didn't even question. So when I *didn't* get pregnant when I was ready, I was surprised and shocked; it had never occurred to me that I wouldn't be able to. Peter would try to pacify me by saying it would eventually happen or if it didn't, we'd simply carry on with our lives, but I wasn't convinced. I don't think men can truly understand the biological need that a woman feels. The more I *couldn't* get pregnant, the more panicky I felt.

I started having tests and it was discovered that my body was producing huge amounts of the hormone you normally produce when you're breastfeeding. Prolactin. How weird was that? Why it was doing this became an interesting argument between two specialists, which I will talk about a little later. The upshot was that my body couldn't get pregnant while the levels of prolactin were so high; it turns out breastfeeding is nature's way of saying, *Let's not have another baby quite yet.* So, I was put on some medication that takes the levels down, but unfortunately, in my case, it had no effect whatsoever; the levels were still as high as they'd ever been. I was 'breastfeeding' for England.

After a long period of taking medication that wasn't helping, I was scheduled to go to St Bartholomew's Hospital, the leading place for this sort of hormonal problem. I'd been taking my temperature, as you do, when you want to get pregnant and had noticed that my temperature had 'stayed up' after rising at the time of ovulation. This is *usually* an indication that you're pregnant, so I was in the rather bizarre situation of thinking I *may* be pregnant, when I got to the hospital for further investigations (into why I *couldn't* get pregnant). So, I had to say when I arrived, '*I know this is a bit strange but … I think I may be pregnant, so before you do any invasive tests, can you take a look.*'

The upshot was, that despite all the odds, I *was* pregnant and back in 1981, if I'd been anywhere else, I wouldn't have seen it on a scan … but St Bart's had a very advanced machine and there she was – a tiny pinprick of a person. No one could explain *how* I'd got pregnant with such high levels of prolactin, it just seemed like a miracle had taken place. She had battled her way through that torrent of anti-baby hormones, to implant herself in my womb.

I saw two different consultants during these child-bearing years, who had very different opinions. The first one, at St Bart's, said that I *must* have a pituitary gland tumour; there was no other explanation for the high levels of prolactin, even though he couldn't actually *see* one on the scan. It was *definitely* there, apparently. For those who don't know, the pituitary is found at the base of your brain, in line with the top of your nose and is like the 'master commander' of all your hormones. To have a tumour in it or on it, was a major disaster, as you can go blind if it is allowed to grow.

I was in shock.

I had the weird experience of having my eyes checked to see if the tumour was growing, all the way through my pregnancy. As far as I knew, it wasn't. My eyes were okay and it felt very incongruous when all the action was taking place in my abdomen, to have all the 'focus' on my eyes. I was told I would be unable to breastfeed, as it would make the whole situation worse, making the tumour bigger. I can remember feeling sick with worry and wondering where it was all going to lead. For nine months I expected to go blind … but I didn't.

I gave birth to my beautiful daughter after a long, pretty horrible, induced labour. They made me lie on my back the whole time and it felt like my back was going to break in two. But as she emerged, I quickly forgot the pain ... and fell instantly in love. The thorny issue of feeding her, instantly raised its head. I'd been told by a world expert that breastfeeding could make me go blind ... raise the prolactin levels to crazy proportions ... give me terrible breast ulcers ... but here was this gorgeous little girl, needing milk. I decided that I'd give it a try, even though it could be dangerous for me.

Unfortunately, the specialist's words kept ringing in my ears and eventually, I just *couldn't* do it. By this time, however, the milk was flowing and they had to bind my breasts to stop the flow. It was (almost) as painful as childbirth and I'm *not* exaggerating. Agony. It was like having burning rocks attached to my chest.

Of course, bottle feeding was (and is) frowned upon and I was made to feel extremely guilty. It was as if my child would be permanently scarred/disfigured/deprived, as a result of my selfish decision, but I felt like saying, *How would you feel if you were in my shoes, with potential blindness, ulcers and tumours thrown in your face?*

It all, in fact, turned out fine. The baby was as happy as Larry (whoever he is) and it meant that Peter could help with the feeds, which was definitely an added bonus. The consultant was *still* convinced that I had a tumour, despite the fact that everything pointed to him being wrong. Perhaps I'm now in a medical journal somewhere, as a patient who defied the odds.

My abiding memory of my time in an RAF hospital, after the birth, was being made to do PT with a strapping member of the Air Force and being made to push my own bed along a corridor. I'd lost a lot of blood during the birth and was as weak as a baby myself, so the exercises and bed-pushing nearly made me pass out. It feels unbelievable *now* that I was made to do this. Another memory: having not my *own* name at the end of the bed, *but* 'Wife of Flight Lieutenant Knights'. It still affronts me now. If there's *one* time in your life, when you should be acknowledged as a female person in your own right, it's when you've just spent hours in agony, pushing a baby out. The third memory is a nicer one: Peter bringing my first son, Toby, (the Labrador) to the ward door, so that we could see each other. Snow was thick on the ground and I can still visualise them both in the snow.

The strange thing was that having started producing babies, I couldn't stop. I got pregnant again so quickly the second time and this time, a different specialist said, *'Just forget everything about tumours, don't worry about it any more'*. So that's what I did. No more monitoring of my eyesight, no more worries about breastfeeding ... but unfortunately, the first guy had set a seed of doubt in my head and I found his ideas just kept creeping into my brain. So, when my son was born, I made the decision not to breastfeed and it was the right one for me. I stopped taking the medication and simply just forgot that I had a hormonal problem ... and then got pregnant again. The third time, with a slightly larger gap, for another unrelated problem, was just as traumatic.

With two babies *in the bag*, so to speak, I decided that perhaps I didn't want to have another one quite so quickly, so, with what looks like, in hindsight, very bad advice and utter stupidity, I had a coil fitted after two months of giving birth. To the uninitiated, an IUD or intrauterine device, is placed inside the womb to stop further pregnancies. Goodness knows why I went for that option. Now, I think IUDs are barbaric things and would never advise anyone to have one, especially so soon after birth, when your womb is still thin and recovering from carrying a baby.

The result was that when it was inserted, the doctor managed to shove it *straight through the wall of my womb*.

Great.

Just after the insertion, we were due to stay with my sister for the weekend, with our twenty-two month old toddler and two month old baby, in tow. We must have been mad to inflict that on her and her family, but on the drive there, I started to feel terrible. I'd felt bad since the insertion, but had put it down to the procedure. By the time we got to her house, I was doubled up in pain. We went straight to the local hospital, leaving her with our children. Thank God I wasn't breastfeeding, on reflection.

They kept prodding my stomach saying it looked like I had appendicitis. I can remember saying to them, *'Well, it seems like quite a coincidence, as it started at exactly the same time as having a coil put in'* ... but they continued down that route until, at last, they did a scan of some sort and discovered the coil, just about to enter my liver. So, I then had to have a major operation to get it out, with them cutting vertically into my stomach, giving me the equivalent of a hysterectomy wound.

The whole thing was so terrifying and so unnecessary. I look back and wonder why I didn't just take the pill? Probably because, in those days, it wasn't very 'advanced' – it was a much higher dosage than it is today and maybe because I'd had such extreme hormone problems, I didn't want to exacerbate them. Who knows why I made the decision? Now, you can even get the pill without prescription – what progress we've made since then.

My poor sister had to look after two very young children for quite some time; between her and Peter, they managed to overdose the baby with colic medication and panicked that they'd done irreparable damage, but all was okay. My twenty-two month old toddler started calling my sister, Mummy, which I found upsetting and she didn't want to be cuddled by me when she was brought into the hospital to see me. Looking back, I probably looked frightening to her: a pale, listless Mummy lying in a strange bed.

When we eventually got home, the wound caused all sorts of problems; it didn't heal and I had a haematoma which lasted weeks. The whole thing was a complete nightmare; I was even told I couldn't pick up the baby – not easy when you have a baby who needs feeding, changing etc. so I had to employ an au pair. She was a lovely Italian girl but she became so fond of him, I had to ask *her* when I wanted to hold my own baby.

Just as a side note, I remember thinking she was really weird because she put olive oil on everything. Back in the eighties in England, nobody was using olive oil; the sight of her dipping bread into it, was just *peculiar*. How times change. I can't live without it now.

You'd think this would have put me off the whole *children* thing, but the human desire to replicate itself has a strange power. I know I already had two children, a girl and a boy, the perfect pair ... but I can remember thinking, *this isn't complete.* I *knew* there was one more; it was just a feeling which I've never been able to explain. And low and behold in 1986, I gave birth to another girl and my family immediately felt *whole*.

Everything was fine this time; the doctors were worried that because I had this relatively recent scar on my stomach, that somehow giving birth would make it split (what a ghastly thought) so I had to go to Bath hospital, an hour away, to give birth. We were driving down a country lane at one in the morning, with me in labour, and a deer jumped in front of us. Peter did an emergency stop and I can remember saying something along the lines of *I could do without that excitement* but it was probably a lot more expletive-ridden. The hospital was very busy – there were two sets of twins being born that night – so, when my baby arrived safely, I was left to my own devices; there just wasn't the staff. I suppose they reckoned that a third-time mum could get on with it without help, but it was still a shock to have someone so small to look after – she was only just over six pounds.

They transferred me to the local hospital the next day, where I had very different treatment. *'You stay there, dear, we'll deal with baby. You go back to sleep'.* It was marvellous. I really didn't want to go home when the time came; I knew I had a five year old, a two and a half year old and a husband, waiting for me.

Only five months later, Peter was sent to the Falklands for four months.

That was a difficult time. Enough said.

But what a strange decade that was for me, the eighties. Trying to get pregnant and failing miserably because of some obscure hormone problem that no one else had ever *heard* of and which made me feel a bit of a freak. Then, *getting* pregnant under strange circumstances which felt like magic. Then ... getting pregnant *again* rather too quickly and then, what are the chances? Some doctor nearly killing me, by trying to *stop* me having babies. You couldn't really make that up; it's like something out of a rather badly-written TV drama.

Lessons to be learned from this: never give up on your dreams of having babies, it might happen one day, despite the odds. Breastfeeding isn't the be-all and end-all of everything. (I have three healthy adult children, who weren't affected by my decision) and ... *don't* put metal devices inside a soft body part.

CHAPTER 7

"After a while, you just want to be with the one that makes you laugh." —Chris Noth as Mr. Big, Sex and the City

Akrotiri 1991 – 1994

I'll always remember that day.

Peter rang and announced casually, *"I've been offered a posting to Cyprus. What do you think?"*

I was in Cornwall at the time; we'd been together on holiday, until the RAF kindly called him in, due to the worsening situation in the Middle East; it was 2nd August, 1990 and Iraq had invaded Kuwait. To be fair, my friend's husband, who wasn't in the military, but in the City, also left in a hurry, as the stock market was going nuts. Us girls made the tough decision to stay put with our five children and stoically continue our holiday, without our men. The weather was beautiful and we were enjoying some female time together, letting the kids run riot on the beach, while we looked on, in a half-hearted way. Our cottage overlooked a beautiful sandy beach where the sea went out for miles, so they could play safely at low tide, without too much of our attention.

"Oh my God. Just like that? A posting in the Med, without any warning?"

"Well, yes. I thought you'd be pleased? It's that or High Wycombe."

The enormity of the conversation was hitting me. I was silent at my end, while I weighed up the pros and cons of both scenarios: if we went to Cyprus, on the one hand, I could give up my teaching job (which, as you've already heard, I hated), but on the other hand, it was leaving everything that was familiar behind and stepping out into the unknown; if we went to High Wycombe, it would mean selling the house and moving our lives or living apart during the week.

"When?" I said, heart thumping.

"We'd probably have to leave the UK after Christmas, so we've got a few months to plan."

"Can I think about it? It's not something I can just say yes to …"

"Yes … I'll ring again tomorrow and you can tell me your answer then."

Oh, so twenty-four hours to decide whether to totally change my entire life, then?

The situation in the Middle East was also something

to consider. Would I be taking the kids into a war zone? A quick glance at an old globe in the cottage, confirmed the proximity of Cyprus to danger. Did I really want to swop our peaceful existence for a prolonged holiday in the sun, with bombs thrown in?

As we lay on our sun-beds watching the kids, it seemed like an impossible decision to make: sun versus rain; hot climate versus cold; employment versus no work; friends and family versus strangers; own home versus married quarters. The two older children were settled in school, the youngest was soon to start.

But then ... this could be my life *every* day ... lying on a sun-bed, instead of being stuck in a classroom teaching the joys of Shakespeare to unwilling thirteen year olds. The more I thought about it, the more it seemed like the *perfect* escape. It would be an amazing opportunity for us all, to experience life in a faraway place, away from the rat race.

"So ... what do you think?" Peter asked, the next day. I could tell he was keen to go.

"Let's do it," I heard myself saying. Even as I said it, I was having doubts, but all things considered, it was the best decision ... for all of us.

There followed months of hardly seeing Peter at all, as he flew continuously out to Cyprus, due to the Iraq situation and he finally left for his posting in February, 1991. I stayed, so that the children could finish their term at school and I had to pack up the house and organise everything, on my own. We eventually went out in April when the ground offensive had finished and the war was effectively over. We travelled on an RAF plane, landing at Akrotiri on a warm, sunny April day. I had, in fact, visited Cyprus once before for a holiday, but this was something quite different: this was the start of a whole new life.

It was a daunting prospect in *so* many ways. The only person I knew on the camp was Peter. The children were starting new schools; we were to live in a married quarter, which turned out to be a house straight out of the 1950's; we were going to have to survive for at least six weeks without any of our things from home. But having got over the initial shock, the sun did its magic and with the children on their school holidays, we spent our time on the camp's many beaches, swimming in the sea. No one else was down there; only people who'd arrived from the UK would venture to the beach clubs, so early in the year. To us, it was like a perfect, English summer; to seasoned 'veterans', it was cold and the sea temperature was far too low for swimming.

Slowly but surely, I began to meet people, the kids settled in with the surprisingly familiar English school system and life took on this rather relaxed and with hindsight, idyllic pace: very early starts, the school day over by 1 pm and the afternoons on the beach: windsurfing, swimming, water-skiing and lolling around. Peter was in charge of the airfield, which was surprisingly busy, but he too could spend his afternoons on the beach, with the occasional call to oversee an aircraft coming in, late. I can still see him now, on a wind-surfer, fag in his mouth, sunglasses on, sailing out to sea, without a care in the world.

The children began to look like adverts for healthy cereals, with their ash blond hair, mahogany skin and a sprinkling of freckles. Their life was like something out of an Enid Blyton book: the freedom of the fifties and sixties, wrapped up in sunshine. None of us in the quarters worried about where they were, as the camp was completely secure. Their friends all lived within walking distance and they wandered from house to house, cycled to school and played on the bondu, surrounding the houses. They'd go to the outdoor swimming pool for swimming lessons or to the beach for sailing and windsurfing lessons. All that was missing was Timmy, the dog, for their adventures. We did, however, acquire Oliver, the ginger rescue cat, who was nearly as good.

Us adults also lived lives that harked back to the past. We all reverted to being *young and stupid* again. We were only in our late thirties/early forties anyway, so we weren't very old, but before we'd gone to Cyprus, the responsibility of being parents to three little children had weighed us down, without us realising. Once we were on our Mediterranean paradise island, it was as if we shed an outer layer of skin to reveal those people we'd been pre-children and we both found a new lease of life. Peter bought himself a boat … we bought a snazzy four-by-four car … I seemed to shed a few pounds and got browner than I'd ever been in my entire life. I'd always just turned bright red, peeled and gone white again before, but with constant sun, I found I could tan, which definitely made me feel good.

The social life on the camp was crazy: balls, parties, cocktails, barbecues, boat trips … camp life was geared towards having fun. In those days, everything was so cheap; not only was it cheaper to eat out in Cyprus than in the UK, but on the camp, everything was even cheaper still. It meant we could afford to go out whenever we wanted, with a ready supply of baby-sitters, willing and able to help out. I remember one particular 'run' when we went out thirteen nights on the trot. The mind boggles now; we can hardly cope with one night a week these days and that's getting home at 11.30, at the latest. On so many occasions, I remember walking home as the sun was beginning to rise and the birds were starting to twitter in the trees.

So, did it all live up to expectations?

I certainly didn't have to work out there, as wives in those days weren't allowed to. This simply made my mind *even* clearer that I never wanted to step foot in a school *ever* again. The children had the most incredible time; they learned so many new skills, the school was excellent and to this day, that time defines their childhood.

I, too, learned new skills: windsurfing became a

favourite hobby (but for years afterwards, I regretted it, as I ended up with an awful back problem). I learned to water-ski which, for me, was quite a feat. Peter became very proficient at water-skiing, being able to mono-ski and show-off to us lesser mortals. He also became a snow ski instructor, played loads of tennis and any other sport that was available.

I loved my time there: I fell in love with the island, the food, the landscape ... but I was ready to come home, in the end. What I hadn't realised was that each year was a repeat of the one before: the same balls, the same parties. Friends you'd made, left and got posted back to the UK and by the third year, I began to notice it. It was time to move on, to get back to 'real life'. The life we'd led there wasn't real, but it was heaven while it lasted.

For those of you who've read my books, you'll probably have already noticed the parallels with my first novel, *Aphrodite's Child*. When we there, I realised what a good setting RAF Akrotiri was for a women's fiction novel. It had all the elements: an exotic setting, the military, family turmoil, isolation from friends and family ... but it wasn't until I started my MA in Creative Writing in 2012, that I started weaving Emily's story into a dramatic plot.

I can honestly say that Cyprus has had a profound effect on us all. We even bought a house there and still own it. We don't get out there as much as we'd like; Peter wanted to move there in retirement but ... I didn't. It's always been a bit of a bone of contention between us. I love it there, but I wouldn't want to *live* there again and that's the difference.

There are too many things and people I'd miss in England. It seems strange, but having spent three years in the sun, I really missed the English seasons. In some ways, it's great to know for sure that tomorrow will be sunny, but after a while, I longed for the wonderful English spring full of cow parsley and buttercups; the warmth of summer drizzle and the autumnal colours. There's a limit to how many days I want to lie in the sun and look at the sea.

It's not real life … and the sun gave us both cancer.

CHAPTER 8

"Love is a temporary madness. It erupts like volcanoes and then subsides. And when it subsides, you have to make a decision. You have to work out whether your roots have so entwined together that it is inconceivable that you should ever part. Because this is what love is." —Louis de Bernières

My 'Other' Careers – 1991 Onwards

I've been doing photography for years now but again, it was something that I took up later in life and 'fell into'.

I'm not sure where the interest came from, although my father had huge amounts of slides back in the day, so maybe it was from him. I can remember getting my first proper camera and becoming obsessed. It was around the time of having babies, so they sparked this interest in me that had lain dormant or even dead, for years. It was when film cameras were still in operation, so my drawers became crammed full of negative strips, which I kept (but which I recently chucked out, in a big clear out). I wanted to document every aspect of our lives and I have many photo albums to prove it. In those days, you weren't sure if you'd got anything worth keeping until you got the film back, so it was always exciting to open the package of new prints.

I did loads of studying about how to take good pictures, learning the difference between an f stop and a shutter speed and an ISO speed and I began to see good results. I went on portrait photography courses, bought loads of books and regularly read photography magazines. Gradually, it all began to make sense and I could get the settings right, on the go ... just. Taking pictures for fun of my own children was one thing, but then I branched out and started taking pictures for money. A very different ball game.

I'd started on a small scale in Cyprus, but it wasn't until we came back to the UK and bought our current house, that I started doing it seriously. It was nerve-wracking and I had to pretend I had much more confidence than I really did. We changed the room above our garage into a studio, which was ideal in every way – apart from the height, the width and the length, ha ha, but I had to make do with what I had. I began to buy more and more *stuff:* studio lights, backdrops, remote controls, lenses, hoods – you name it, I had it. I began to advertise, print business cards and eventually made a website. Peter was, as always, very supportive and helped me set it all up.

It sounds as if this happened quickly, but it took place over years, between children, teaching, running a house and a life. I realised I enjoyed meeting new people and interacting with them, but it was sometimes challenging, to say the least. You had to make it all seem *dead easy*, seamless and friendly, covering up the fact that some technical glitch has just happened: one of the lights had stopped working; your batteries were dead; you forgot to bring the vital lens to an outdoor shoot. It was important to smile and appear totally calm, even though your outdoor shoot was getting rained on, or you couldn't find the key to your studio.

The people were, of course, the all-important part of the picture and the moment they turned up at the studio, I would get a pretty good idea about how the photos would turn out. There would be the over-anxious mother; the screaming baby; the hyper-active toddler; the bored-looking teenager; the boisterous dog (yes, they were often part of the proceedings too); the angry dad, trying not to show how fed up he was ... or maybe a combination of all of the above. The variety was endless. My job was to get all these people into a small space and cajole them into spending at least an hour together, looking as if they were enjoying the process.

If I was lucky, I might catch Little Johnny smiling at the camera, without Dad's clenched, white-knuckled hand holding him down, showing in the picture. Or

Baby Grace, looking all sweet and innocent, before throwing up curdled milk all over Mummy's shoulder. If I was *really* lucky, I might catch the family group of six looking at the camera at the same time, with their eyes open and appearing to like each other, without appearing to be starry-eyed robots.

It's so important that a group of people link together naturally: the six year old leaning against Dad's leg; the ten year old snuggling nicely under Mum's arm and Mum and Dad standing close together and everyone looking like they're a *unit*. Stray hands can completely ruin a picture – a hand resting on a shoulder, seemingly from nowhere, or gripping a waist, can appear alien, or threatening. I found some people automatically gelled together and looked natural; others looked as if there were magnets between them, forcing them apart.

All the elements have to be assessed in a second: eyes open, tick; smiles, tick; nice grouping, tick. Most of the time it was more like this: somebody's just fucking blinked, tick; that little shit on the end, just pulled a face, tick; the baby looks as if it's doing a poo, tick; Mum looks as if she's about to cry, tick. The toddler's just crawled out of the picture. Bloody tick. But people, on the whole, loved the pictures I took and I began to build up a good little business. I wasn't ever going to make a fortune at it, but it paid a few bills (mainly for my new equipment, much to Peter's dismay).

I found studio portraits, the most stressful type

of photography. There was more room for technical problems and the sheer size of my studio encouraged antipathy between people. It was like being in a room full of people being put under huge amounts of stress – no, it wasn't *like* that, it actually *was* that.

I preferred the 'natural' outdoor shoots. So much more room to walk or run about, so much more air to breathe. Less worry about the technical side of lighting – just the sun to think about ... and the rain. In theory, it would be children running gaily through fields of dandelions, sitting on bridges over rivers, or leaning against gates and sitting on walls, with the sun's golden hour spreading an orange hue to the sky. In practice, it was trying to get the shot before the child fell over in said dandelions and stung itself on stingy nettles; or someone slipping down into the water and drowning and/or falling off the wall and breaking a leg.

I often tried to get those *just walking towards the camera* shots, where the family looked genuinely relaxed and happy, as if they were out for a Sunday stroll. These usually worked well and with a bit of Photoshop, could be made to look timeless. I just hoped the family didn't remember that it *actually* took about ten 'takes' of walking casually towards the camera, to get the one good shot.

It wasn't just families I did shoots for; I had business people wanting head shots: women would want to look glamorous, professional and approachable and men just wanted to look ... manly. I took shots of martial arts teachers, a yoga teacher, potential models, musicians, pop bands, pet dogs ... you name it, I took pictures of it.

The two weirdest ones I did were, one guy who had a phobia of having his picture taken and who was trying to overcome it ... not very successfully, as it turned out. And another guy who sent me pictures beforehand, of his penis (I ended up saying I was too busy). He was *way* before his time with his dick pics; he must be in his element now.

I also did events: children's parties; wedding anniversaries; old people's birthdays; family get-togethers; christenings and pony club meetings. I would get ridiculously nervous before each one, but on the whole, they were okay. They made me think I could cope with weddings. Big mistake.

Wedding photography is a whole different thing. It's someone's special day, one that they'll remember for the rest of their lives and you're the one tasked to make the memories. I'm not sure why I did this; maybe I thought it would be more lucrative. On paper, it *was*, but in practice, you got about two pounds an hour. What I hadn't factored in was the meetings, phone calls and home visits – and that was *before* the wedding had even taken place.

A typical conversation with a couple would go like this:

"So ... what kind of pictures are you hoping to get from the wedding?"

"Well, we *love* those sort of relaxed ... romantic ... dreamy ... journalistic shots ... nothing staged. Not the traditional wedding photos."

"So, you *don't* want pictures of your parents with you, then?"

"Oh, yes ... maybe the parents ..."

"And what about the bridesmaids ... the extended family ..."

"Yes, well, we'd definitely want shots of *them*, yes. Just a few."

"So, you *do* want the groups, then?"

"Yes."

This *literally* happened every time. Everyone *thought* their wedding was so unique, so different from everyone else's but, in fact, they were all exactly the same, but with different dresses, in a variety of venues and with a different cake. They all *thought* they wanted unique photos ... but they all wanted exactly the same. I began to find the process somewhat repetitive and annoying: the *getting ready* shots, the '*I do*' shots, the *group* shots, the *speech* shots, the *cutting of the cake* shots, the *first dance* shots. I thought I might eventually lose my mind.

And the strange thing was, the more you did weddings, the more terrifying they became. Once I'd downloaded the pictures onto a hard drive and they were little thumbnails on my computer, so to speak,

I could relax, although thoughts like this...*what if the hard drive goes wrong and I can't retrieve the photos* kept me awake at night. What if my hard drive *and* computer caught fire? Should I back up the files somewhere else too? This was before the 'cloud' and the certainty that your files were safe, somewhere in cyber space. The thought of losing a couple's big day was really quite disturbing.

Until the files were safe, my body ached with tension all day – and what a *long* day it was. Celebrity culture has a lot to answer for – most brides think they are celebs these days and want a photographer to follow them around from the moment they get up. First, to shoot the riveting hair and make-up session; then, the dress hanging on the door, the shoes and bags laid artistically on the bed. The bride and bridesmaids drinking champagne on the bed, the bride and mother of the bride hugging by the front door ... by the time you've actually got to the wedding, you're completely knackered; it could be a good twelve-hour day of running around.

Peter came with me as my 'assistant' to a few weddings and it was an interesting thing to observe. Most people assumed *he* was the photographer and *I* was the assistant. Bloody cheek. He became good at snatching candid shots of people, while I did the expected shots, the ones that couldn't be missed.

Then, there would be the follow up meetings, the post production, the choices, the editing, the books, the CD's, the prints, the USB. Every bride would want a book of the wedding (in theory) but often the pictures would stay on the USB forever, as married life got in the way of *actually* trying to decide which pictures should go in the book.

I gather now brides also employ social media people who just use their phones to take pictures for Instagram. I'm so *pleased* I gave it up – that would be *so* annoying to deal with: you're trying to get '*the*' shot and some other person is vying with you and probably stepping into the shot. It was bad enough having old uncle Jim with his Pentax getting in your way, never mind some mobile phone-brandishing-Insta-influencer type.

I realised that portrait photography was better paid and far less stressful, so in the end, I opted only to do that. But as time has gone on, I've done less and less photography and my business has wound down and down, to a full stop. I didn't want all the stress that went with shoots and I felt as *if I'd been there, done that.*

Recently, in 2023, I've cancelled my photography website (after a lot of thought) and I'm selling all my equipment; it's lost its allure. I find writing is the thing I want to spend my time doing, but I still love taking photos for myself. I've bought the best mobile phone money can buy and the photos I take on it are great. As I'm glued to my phone, it's always available and I can click away, whenever I want to. I drive Peter mad; whenever we're out walking, I'm always looking for 'the shot'. I laugh with him because he and

Mabel often wander into the stunning landscape I'm trying to take, without realising. If we go somewhere new, like Lisbon, for example, I know I'm annoying to be with, as I 'see' photos all the time and have a compulsion to take them. All that I do with them now is stick them on my Insta stories these days, though, so I suppose it's all a bit pointless, but I enjoy it. My mobile phone photography has made me even more attached to my phone and it was pretty important before. I love my phone because it's light, convenient and always on my person, which is more than can be said for my heavy Canon.

#

One thing I will categorically blame Peter for, happened in 1997. When we came back from Cyprus in 1994, he left the Air Force and became a financial advisor. This made a lot of sense, as he was going to join a bank when he was twenty but then got into the Air Force, as mentioned earlier. He has a fantastic brain for numbers, so it was an obvious choice and there were lots of jobs going in that sector. The pay wasn't bad and it meant we could stay in Wiltshire.

Now, I was ready to have a full time job. The kids were all that bit older and I quite fancied earning some money.

One day Peter said, "You'd make a good financial advisor ... you're good at talking to people and that's what it's all about."

I remember saying, "But don't you have to have a

good brain for Maths?" and him replying, "No, it's easy ..."

Famous last words.

I decided to take him up on his idea and found myself suddenly thrust into the world of United Friendly in Bristol. What attracted me to this somewhat weird career change? A good salary ... and a card with which I could fill the car with petrol, for *any* purpose. Never a good idea to follow the money. I started the course and quite quickly felt totally out of my depth. I had to take an exam, *Financial Planning One*, after a while ... the thought of FP Two and FP Three made me feel physically sick.

The whole concept of me being knowledgeable about investments and pensions is now laughable. I had (and still have) zero interest in numbers and/or money, which wasn't a good start. To my credit, I did somehow pass FP One, probably by simply learning everything by rote and working ridiculously hard. I wanted to hold onto my petrol card at all cost – a godsend when you've got three children at three different schools, miles away from your home.

A very strange thing happened to me during my time as a financial whizz kid. I was doing my course in Bristol with a young guy and we both innocently turned up one morning for work, to find the building locked and *literally* no one there. No cars in the car park ... nothing. We couldn't work out what on earth was going on. I started ringing around and asking random strangers, who happened to be passing. It turned out that, overnight, United Friendly's sales force, including me and this other guy, had been taken over by Friends Provident … and no one had thought to tell us. This kind of summed up their attitude to us, we thought. We were told to get on the motorway as quickly as possible and make our way to Gloucester, where we would now be working.

Oh okay then, thanks for that. A totally different city.

In Gloucester, I acquired this awful new boss who nowadays, would be done for misogyny, bullying and anything else you'd like to name. The whole team was male (apart from me) and we'd go out for team lunches where they'd totally ignore me. At least I wasn't sexually harassed.

I began to hate the job.

I'd got to the stage where I had to start seeing *actual* people who wanted advice. Looking back, this was scary, in so many ways. Not only did I *not* know what I was talking about, but I had to go into people's houses, alone.

One particular solitary man sticks in my mind. He wasn't a sexual predator or anything, but he did spend a lot of time talking about his model bus collection and showing me endless pictures of them. I couldn't wait to get out.

Another client accused me of mis-selling something. I was terrified and thought I was going to be sued, but then Peter looked at the documents and said, in his expert opinion, the complaint was '*a load of old bollocks*', and he did tend to know what he was talking about (unlike me).

Needless to say, I eventually gave up the fight and I can remember feeling like a proverbial weight had lifted off my shoulders.

Handing back the petrol card was a bit of a bummer but … life's too short to do a job that keeps you awake at night, even if you get free petrol.

#

TEFL or Teaching English as a Foreign Language seemed like a natural progression from teaching English to school children, who indeed, regarded English as a foreign language, too.

I decided when I got back from Cyprus, that this was to be my next career. I knew a lot about the English language, surely, didn't I?

I enrolled on an intensive course in Cheltenham, which involved a daily round trip of over two hours. It was exhausting and I quickly found out that I didn't know my gerunds from my present participles. How can you speak a language without understanding its structure? Easily, it seems. I could remember being taught parsing as a child (dictionary definition of parsing is: to resolve a sentence into its component parts and describe their syntactic roles). I can recall being totally flummoxed by this and, in fact, if I'd understood it better all those years ago, I might have got on better doing this course.

It was a steep learning curve; we were told we would never look at, or listen to, English the same way again, and boy, was that true. Suddenly, every sentence was fraught with difficulty. You had to tune your brain into a foreigner's brain and I quickly understood how difficult our language is.

English has one of the biggest vocabularies in the world; we've borrowed so many words from Greek and Latin that it is expansive. Just imagine being a speaker of English as a second language, trying to get your head around the 'phrasal verb'. The difference between the meanings of: to look into (something, ie investigate); to look after (someone, ie to care for); to look up to (someone ie admire); to look forward to (something, ie to anticipate something with pleasure). The list goes on and on … and on. To a native speaker, it's obvious, but it's impenetrable to learners. And as for the Conditional – there are four types of conditional sentences and they're all hypothetical situations with possible consequences. Why would I *ever* need one of those, you ask? But you don't realise how many times you say things like, *'If it rains tomorrow, I won't go'* or *'If I'd used my favourite numbers this week, I would have won the lottery.'*

So, having done a few teaching practices with college students, I set off with this new-found wisdom, to teach English to foreign business people. They didn't want to just speak English (oh my god, I've split an infinitive) ... oh no, they wanted to complicate it with business: they wanted to learn how to chair a meeting, make important phone calls, negotiate deals and make presentations. I personally had no idea how to do any of these things, so I had to learn on the job. My one big advantage was that I could speak fluent English and they *couldn't* (that didn't stop one Japanese man telling me I was categorically wrong about a piece of grammar).

I often taught them in small groups of four and there might be four different nationalities in the group. We never spoke their languages, everything had to be conducted in English, from start to finish. It was nearly all speaking and listening, so there was a lot of role-play of negotiations and meetings. I was pretty out of my depth here to begin with, but I learned a lot about business, that's for sure. They came from all sorts of companies: car makers, shipping, supermarkets, financial institutions, to name but a few. On the whole they were lovely people, just desperate to learn so that they could keep their job. They were poles apart from the secondary school kids, who really weren't interested. These people were hyper-keen and literally drained you of all your knowledge. I would get home, incapable of functioning in the evening sometimes. The last thing I wanted to do was to talk to anyone but I met some extremely interesting people in my time doing this job; I also learned a lot about different cultures and lifestyles.

I can always remember the Japanese man who was genuinely upset when it was time to go home. His life in Tokyo was awful, or so it felt to me. He would have to leave his house at 6 am to commute for over an hour, standing all the way to the city and maybe three nights a week, he was expected to go out in the evening and wouldn't get home until 11pm. He lived in a tiny flat and he'd seen a different aspect of life, here in the countryside in England.

There was the German guy who said when I started the conversation rolling with, 'Tell me about your job', who answered, 'I hate my job, can we talk about something else?' I think we ended up talking about motorbikes a lot. There was the Frenchman who was visibly upset, as his wife had left him and taken his daughter to the other end of France. Every weekend this child was put on a plane, so that he could see her. I often felt a bit like a counsellor … but I still corrected their English.

I did this for twelve years, but finally decided I couldn't do it any more. I felt as if I might actually go mad if I continued. I would miss the people I met every week but I wouldn't miss analysing the English language. I still know what a present participle is, but thank God, I don't have the need to know any more. A lasting legacy, though, is a hatred of stray apostrophes, for example, the classic *orange's* and *pear's* in a fruit shop, but I can live with that.

CHAPTER 9

"Being someone's first love may be great, but to be their last is beyond perfect." —Anonymous

Writing … Eventually – 2012 Onwards

We can all blame Peter, again. Poor bloke; he's got a lot to answer for. He was the one who said: *Why don't you do an MA in Creative Writing?* But *this* time, he landed on an idea that was to show me what I *should* have been doing all along.

I'd been moaning on about how bored I was at the time, having finally given up TEFL teaching. I realised that I needed something else to do. So, I applied to Bath Spa university, which, it turned out, was one of the best Creative Writing MA courses in the country and conveniently only twenty-five minutes' drive from our house. The thought of studying again for some reason appealed and terrified me, in equal measure. The one thing that worried me more than anything was whether I'd be the oldest person on the course, but the very first person I met on that first day was considerably older than me (although she didn't look it). Older people were the majority, it turned out. There were some young ones, who'd gone straight from doing a BA to an MA, but most of us were past our prime, but fancying ourselves as the next JK Rowling.

Some of the course tutors were very inspiring, well-established and successful writers: Tessa Hadley and Fay Weldon, Naomi Alderman and Philip Hensher, to name just four. I felt just a *tad* intimidated.

We'd had to submit an idea for a novel and some sample pages and fortunately, they liked my idea, much to my surprise. Having got in, I now had to develop it and submit myself to *positive criticism* on a regular basis.

My original idea was to write a funny, ironic account of my time as an RAF officer's wife, but people on the course didn't really '*get*' it and I found myself changing the whole tone of the book. It became serious and developed into a typical woman's contemporary fiction book, all about a woman's emotional *journey*, with drama, betrayal AND a fatal accident thrown in. I'm not saying I was forced to change it, but that's what happened; it developed its own momentum. I've had a hankering to write something funny ever since; a memoir about marriage seemed like a perfect project for that. You might, however, disagree.

The trouble is, when you read your piece out loud and up to ten people ask you for your reason for writing it like that, you begin to question your own motivations and sanity. I ended up changing the narrator from 'I' to 'she' which transformed it. I could now distance myself from the story and give my protagonist a whole different experience to my own. Hers was very exciting, compared to mine. I changed it again back to 'I' a few years later when I re-wrote the book. They say writing is editing ... how true.

The first time I had to read a piece of my writing out loud, I was so nervous I felt sick. Here were all these super-intelligent people, eyes directed towards me, listening with intensity. Every word I was reading sounded absolutely pathetic in my ears (and in *theirs* probably). It was like a form of torture to someone who's got no self-confidence and whose writing had always been a secret pastime.

Once I had got over the initial shock, however, I began to enjoy these sessions and actually looked forward to them. You had to accept that some people wouldn't like your writing and that some could be downright direct in their criticism but, on the whole, we were all in the same boat and most of us tried to be positive, rather than negative. I enjoyed listening to and reading the other students' work too, but I was always *comparing* myself to them. I was trying to write quite a simple story, not one that would tax people's intellects too much and I thought that some of the others were more 'academic' and highbrow than me;

why this should bother me, I don't know. You have to choose the style you're comfortable with in the end, and this is what I did. Writing any long prose is challenging at the best of times.

I studied short stories while I was on the course, which I thoroughly enjoyed. We had to read lots of them, as well write them and I found it fascinating how some writers can draw you in so quickly into another world. I came across Alice Munroe for the first time and absolutely loved her stories; I was so sad to read she's just died (I'm editing this piece in May 2024). We would be asked to write short stories based on a theme and I can remember feeling proud when Tessa Hadley really praised one of mine …

But the main focus was on the novel and the upshot was, I finished the book.

Yay!

Then what?

#

I think we all thought that, as we'd done a Creative Writing MA at a prestigious university, we'd become famous novelists overnight; well, I momentarily did (not become a famous novelist, unfortunately, but *thought* I would). We'd just send off our manuscripts to a few literary agents and within weeks, the offers would come flooding in. We'd be fighting them off with sticks, negotiating vast sums of money and speaking to Steven Spielberg about the film rights. Not only that, Netflix would be on the phone, begging us to be allowed to make our books into the next must-watch series. There'd be a bidding war.

Unfortunately, none of the above happened to any of us, surprisingly; the reality was somewhat different. There were a couple of really clever people who wrote worthy, literary books who got offered deals, but as far as I know, the rest of us didn't. Maybe they did, under pen names?

I'd been to a conference about self-publishing and realised that it was no longer regarded as vanity publishing and that a lot of people were doing it, thanks to Amazon, so I took the plunge ... and did it. At that time, 2013, it wasn't as usual as it is now and I felt like a bit of a rebel, but the thought of being in total control of my writing, my book and my cover, really appealed to me. I was pretty good with technical things, so the whole process of preparing a manuscript to upload to Amazon, creating a cover and marketing it to social media, didn't faze me at all; in fact, I grew to love that side of writing. At about that same time, I went to a lecture by an author, who told us that her publishing company insisted on her having a dead woman on her cover, even though there wasn't a dead woman in her story, *because women sell books*. I thought this was so outrageous *and* ridiculous that it made my decision to 'go solo' even clearer.

Over the years, I've come to the conclusion that literary agents are a pain in the bum, to be honest. (I think I've scuppered my chances of getting a deal from any random agents reading this, ha ha). After I initially went down the self-publishing route, I still hankered for a traditional deal and would send off manuscripts occasionally. I'd just written my fifth novel (I never realised I had so much to say) and I thought, maybe, just maybe, I should try to get an agent, *this* time. So, with my excel spreadsheet set up in an efficient way, I went about sending off lots of submissions. I'd done my research: there are thousands of agents out there and all you have to do is find one who *might* like your book; it's no good sending women's popular fiction to someone looking for the latest sci-fi fantasy, involving vampire robots. So my spreadsheet was full of potential people who stated that they were looking for my kind of story.

Each one set out their 'wish list' of the type of thing they were after and when I found one who appeared to fit the bill exactly, I fantasised that … *This is the one, she'll reply within days …* but of course, they didn't. My submission went off into the ether, never to be seen again. Gone without trace. At first, I sat anxiously waiting for their reply, but after a few months, I'd forgotten I had even sent them.

Each submission had to be very slightly different: *This* agent wanted the first *three* chapters and a *one* page synopsis, *in the body* of the email, with the added threat of, '*Any attachments will be immediately deleted*'. *This* one, however, wanted the first *thirty* pages, a *two* page synopsis with them, *added as attachments*. Another one didn't want a synopsis at all … and only the first *ten* pages.

OH, FOR F***'S SAKE.

My computer was now full of different little bits of novel; short, long and medium synopses and endless attempts at writing emails that didn't make me sound like a complete knob. Honestly, it drove me nuts.

I think there is a secret conspiracy of agents, whose sole purpose is to *piss you off.* (They belong to the same gang that design software, to annoy Peter). And … as for them telling me which bloody pronoun they preferred … it would have been nice to *hear* from them, never mind whether they're a *he* or a *she*. Some said, *you will hear from us in the next twelve weeks,* or some such twaddle. Others said, *due to the volume of submissions, we can't reply to everyone, so if you don't hear from us …* Blah, blah, blah.

I decided I was too *old* to wait for them to deign to get in touch. Time was marching on and the thought of wondering if I'd *ever* hear from one of these people, made me want to shoot myself. I'd heard that even if you got an offer, the publishers would want you to have a well-established social media following and expect you to do most of your own marketing. Surely, that's what you're hoping *they'll* do for *you*? Unless your name is JoJo Moyes or Victoria Hislop, they spend very little of their own money and if your book doesn't sell quickly, they drop you like a stone and your books are pulped. *No thanks.*

One agent did show a tiny bit of interest and asked

for the rest of my manuscript. That was years ago now and when I wrote and asked politely if she'd decided one way or the other, she never replied.

So, I officially gave up.

Fortunately, self-publishing has moved on apace recently. Now there are self-published millionaires; authors on Tik-Tok (or *Book-Tok* as it's known in the self-publishing world) are actually changing the face of the publishing industry and shaking it up. About time too. I read that self-published authors are indeed making more money than traditional authors now.

There are a huge number of companies devoted to helping self-publishers with everything from formatting, to promotion, to editing etc. but I've done it mainly without help and I have to say, I'm glad I made the decision I did, otherwise, I'd still be waiting … and waiting.

I've decided I must be a bit of a control freak when it comes to writing. I want to do *exactly* what I want to do and write what I want to write. I'm sure agents would laugh me out of court about this, but … let them.

CHAPTER 10

"A great marriage is not when the 'perfect couple' comes together. It is when an imperfect couple learns to enjoy their differences." —Dave Meurer

Imagine Us Meeting Now …

I often ponder this situation: what would Peter and I think of each other, if we met now? Forgetting the last fifty-three years. So … in my mind, we're both single, for whatever reason … and some friends decide to introduce us. It's hard to imagine; perhaps we've been *set up* at a dinner party, or we're in a noisy pub. I'm wearing something that I think makes me look young and attractive; I've had my hair cut, make-up's on and I'm even wearing some dangly earrings. I've squirted my favourite perfume each side of my neck and on my wrists.

Let's go for the dinner party scenario. I've arrived on time and I have no idea I'm being set up; I just know that they've invited someone I don't know. We all get a drink and nibble on some nuts. We know each other well and the chat is easy. Then there's a ring on the door and my friend goes to let the mystery guest in … and it's Peter. I can hear muffled conversation and some laughter and then, in he comes. He's late, but has some excuse about his car, watch, computer … take your pick.

I see a bloke of indeterminate age, maybe seventy; a bit overweight, but aren't we all? He hasn't made a huge effort to look smart; he's thrown on a pair of trousers, a shirt without a tie and he has a clean, yet decidedly old-looking pair of brown shoes on his feet. He hasn't shaved for at least four days, the grey stubble is speckled on his face but it somehow manages to look good on him. He's got nice eyes and he laughs easily. His hair is neat, silver grey in a short style, but he's got lots of it, which is unusual for a man his age. That's a good start; I don't like bald men.

How does he see me? Seventy, give or take a decade or two. Hair that is cut in a modern way and still has blond streaks, but is now a weird mixture of grey, blond and brown. I've made an effort to look smart, but I'm not exactly love's young dream, or Joan Collins, Helen Mirren or Twiggy, let's be honest.

What would we make of each other now?

I think we'd talk easily, laugh a lot and ask each other all the right questions, but whether it would 'go anywhere' is a strange thought. Depending on our circumstances, it would be very hard to let someone into your life at our age.

The thing is about growing old *together* is that you remember (just) how your husband/wife *used* to look. You have the photos to prove it: the slim bikini shot by the pool; the cool, long-haired, leather-jacketed lad on a motor bike, with the Mediterranean in the background. Then, the gradual transformation … the smart uniformed servicemen at his passing out parade; the wedding day when the groom looks like a teenager. The pregnant woman in a dress that looks more like a tent, with a toddler by her side; the athletic young dad, running across a beach with three children. The sun-tanned family surrounded by palm trees; the teenagers in Disney, Florida and then the proud parents at the children's weddings. In this 'only just met you' scenario, we could show each other pictures of our past, but it wouldn't mean much as they're someone else's memories. But when you've grown old together, you've seen each other transmogrify, (I love that word) and become the person you share your life with. Every shared memory, every triumph, every joy, every tragedy is etched in those photos and in the lines on each other's faces. And you accept it. You have no other choice. This total stranger, the one you met a million years ago at a tennis club, has shared your life with you and you've arrived at a destination neither one of you could have imagined when you set out. The children have left home and all you have left is each other … but you understand the journey you've both been on. You were there, living it. You're still together and that, in itself, is a miracle.

On paper, we don't have much in common. If we were on an old codgers dating app, against interests I'd put: reading, writing, photography, music, theatre, film, swimming, animals (particularly dogs). Peter would put: rugby, tennis, cricket, golf ... sport, sport and sport and ... maybe DIY. Maybe that's a bit mean; nowadays, he'd add Advanced Sudoku; Wordle and gardening. On paper, we wouldn't be matched at all ... I'd probably reject him out of hand, if I saw his 'likes' but we've got a whole life in common now: children, houses, pets and above all, memories.

And we've actually grown more *alike* – he reads far more than he used to; I watch a bit of sport now, whereas I hated it in the past. I even confess to quite liking football, after having watched *Beckham* on Netflix. (I know, I know, that's hardly an admission of football fandom but I'm getting there). My obsession with dogs has rubbed off on him over the years and he admits a dog is good for getting us out and about. In fact, he's often soppier with Mabel than I am.

And did you know that as men get older, they lose some of their testosterone and women's oestrogen levels drop? Your hormone levels become quite similar. Men become less aggressive and a woman gets less compliant. Not sure about that piece of information when I hear him shouting at some poor, unsuspecting call centre person ... but we definitely argue less than we used to. We used to fight and yell *a lot* when we were younger, but now I don't think either of us can be bothered. It's too much like hard work. But maybe we're just melding and melting into each other? Soon we'll be like one person; the need to communicate will have completely disappeared. We'll know what each other is thinking at all times and any conversation between us will be meaningless.

Actually, maybe that's happened already?

CHAPTER 11

"Husband secretly lowers the thermostat and I secretly turn it back up. We both vehemently deny touching it. Marriage is fun." —Stephanie Ortiz

Home – September, 2022

So, what have we learned so far?

Two people, living harmoniously together (almost) with a dog. They watch TV and walk. They used to have busy lives.

Today, is sunny and warm for the time of year. Indeed, the *whole* of this year has been evidence of global warming. So hot in the summer that the grandchildren were jumping through the garden sprinkler to keep cool; barbecues and eating outside were a regular occurrence. Peter wore his ageing shorts every day and had a *real* reason for wearing his sunglasses and I even bought a fan in from the studio, that was once used to blow a model's hair in a fashion-shoot type way. England took on a Mediterranean feel, everyone looked happy, tanned and relaxed.

And then ... Liz Truss got elected on 5th September, 2022. And then ... the Queen died on 8th September. And then ... Liz and Kwasi had their mini budget. And then ... and then ... inflation went up, mortgages went up, the cost of living soared, scaremongering increased, the media went mad. Kwasi was sacked; Suella was sacked; Liz was ousted and then we got Rishi, the billionaire Asian ex Chancellor, 'a steady pair of hands'.

And boy, did we need a pair of those. For a period there, it was as if Great Britain had seriously lost *all* its marbles. Being a great news watcher, I was glued to it. The journalists were more and more baffled, exasperated and incredulous. Robert Peston became increasingly bonkers and Tom Bradby on the ITV News at Ten, was almost speechless (although that would have been a strange news broadcast). I love those news items when they interview 'the man in the street' in some random town or city, about what's going on. I suppose they think they're doing the viewer a service by getting 'normal' people's views, instead of Oxford-educated media types, but ... do we really need to hear that Christine from Durham is '*disgusted*' by the '*goings* on' in Westminster, or Stan from a barbershop in Leeds thinks the fact that Rishi's shoes are worth more than his house, is a *disgrace*? I often wonder what I would say if I was accosted in the street. I'm sure I'd sound as moronic as the next person.

We're particularly angry at Liz, for personal reasons. We'd discussed for about ten years whether to update our kitchen or not. Every conversation had gone along the same lines:

ME: Let's rip out the kitchen. It's the original one that's been here since the house was built in 1992.

PETER: I hate the utility room. Let's rip that out too.

ME: But I want a utility room.

PETER: Why?

ME: I want the washing machine etc in there.

PETER: The kitchen's too dark. Let's just take down the wall.

ME: Can you imagine living here when all this construction work is being done?

PETER: Let's also take down the wall between the kitchen and dining room.

ME: It's going to cost a bloody fortune.

PETER: Maybe we should build an extension?

ME: The house is already too big for us. We ought to downsize, not upsize.

As I said, we've had a similar conversation to the one above, on a loop, for about ten years. We'd *finally* decided *not* to do any of it and sell the place, in order to downsize. We put the house on the market and BANG … Liz decides to go for *growth, growth, growth* and the housing market goes completely *dead, dead, dead.* Thanks for that, Liz.

So now, we have the house on the market and the big dilemma about when to take it off again. Liz is now confined to the annals of history, interminably appearing in video clips extolling the virtues of *pork markets* and talking about *cheese imports. That-is-a-disgrace.*

Well, Liz, what you did was a disgrace and you've totally scuppered our plans. So we're stuck now, wondering what to do, into eternity.

We love our house though and have lived in it since 1994. Our kids have grown up here and we've celebrated many happy Christmases, Easters and birthdays in it. Long, loud meals, around the very table I'm typing on. Pets have lived here, grown old here and even died here. It's full of memories that drift around in the ether of the rooms and fly through my mind. The walls are covered in photos: some of them of gatherings when all the children and grandchildren came home.

Home. Is it a place or concept? I heard a great saying the other day: *Home is where you long to leave when you're young and yearn to be back in when you're old.*

It's hard to imagine living anywhere else now, but I'm sure one day, we will. It won't be as big, but it will still be a place to call *home*. It just won't have the memories. I often think it would be good to have a new start, to be somewhere where it has always been just Peter and me. When you live in the *family* home, you can't help being aware of the *absence* of your children. You wouldn't want them to still be with you; you want them to go and make their own lives, but … it's still the emptiness of their bedrooms that make you realise they've gone for good. You still refer to their rooms by their names, they still have belongings in there, their presence hovers forever around. Happy memories that now bring tears to the mother without her children.

So, yes, it's time to move on, to face whatever the future has in store for us.

So, thanks Liz. I read in The Times this morning, that you've always been a contrarian, someone who takes the opposite view to most people. Someone who won't take advice and who freezes out people who disagree with you. Well, that really paid off for you, didn't it?

I did suggest to Peter that he and Liz have quite a lot in common; I found it very funny. He did laugh a *little* bit, as I think even *he* realised that being contrary is *maybe* part of his personality. He then proved my point by disagreeing with the Bank of England putting up interest rates today. He's convinced they've done it too late. Maybe he's right, but someone like me always just accepts that people like the Governor of the Bank of England *probably* knows a bit about it.

Not Peter.

CHAPTER 12

"Only married people can understand how you can be miserable and happy at the same time."
—Chris Rock

Us – The Absolute Pleasure Of Going Shopping

Today we're going shopping. This isn't something that we do often; in fact, it's a positively rare experience. I used to shop, but since the pandemic, I do less and less of it. I got used to shopping online during lockdown and now I don't see the need to visit actual buildings, full of *stuff*. Peter has never gone shopping, even when the pandemic was just a film director's dream horror movie.

His idea of going shopping is always: I need shoes. I go to a shop. I choose a pair of shoes. I pay for them. I go home. None of this, wandering around *comparing shoes* nonsense, or this, *buying a different style of shoes from all previous shoes* nonsense. It's just – go in, get them, get out as quickly as possible, as if the shop is about to explode. You're lucky if you're in town for more than forty minutes. This *can* work to my advantage, as, if I'm trying to buy something, I might well end up with a much more expensive item than if I'd gone on my own, because he just wants to get the hell out of there.

So, today, we both desperately need shoes. They are one item I won't buy online; I've got what can only be described politely as *unfortunate* feet. I need to try them on and hobble about in the shop, looking at my feet in those rather strange low-slung mirrors.

We set off at a civilised hour, 11 a.m., after a leisurely lie in bed, a leisurely breakfast and a leisurely walk with Madam (as I call Mabel). It wasn't very leisurely for her; I threw the ball a thousand times to wear her out, as I knew we were leaving her for the morning. When we started putting on our coats and collecting the car keys, she gave us a filthy look and slumped into her bed, in the depths of despair. Anyone would think she's constantly left on her own, but the truth is, she's hardly *ever* alone and therefore hates it when we have the audacity to leave the house without her. She can hardly bear to look at us, never mind say goodbye.

We drive to the nearest shopping mall, a huge place that looks like a cathedral to the modern-day religion of shopping. It's surrounded by shops ranging from supermarkets, to DIY stores to car franchises. There's also a cinema, a bowling alley and numerous fast food outlets. If I didn't know I was in the the south west of England, I'd think I was in America.

"So much for the cost of living crisis," says Peter, as he drives around the car park, scowling.

"People have got to shop," I say. "Anyway, there are plenty of parking spaces, what's the problem?"

"I don't want to park next to someone."

"What?"

"I don't want to park next to some arsehole."

"Why would they necessarily be an arsehole?" I wonder, innocently.

"They'll scratch the car with their doors."

I keep quiet. There's no point arguing with him when he says things like this. According to Peter, everyone else in any car on the road, is either a total wanker or, has been already discussed, a complete arsehole. We cruise around for a few minutes before he realises that it's going to be nigh on impossible to park with nobody either side. He starts manoeuvring into a 'mother and baby' space.

"Peter, you can't park here," I say, bracing myself for the backlash. "We blatantly haven't got a baby," I try to point out.

"They're all empty and they have much wider spaces."

"Yes, but that's the *whole* point; it's so that mothers

and babies have more space and they're near the mall."

"You're a mother," he says.

"Oh, for *God's* sake …"

This has happened many times before, often in disabled spaces. This is one thing (one of many) he objects to.

"They hog all the spaces near the shops and they're always empty," is his perennial argument. Once, he left me sitting in an open-topped car for about fifteen minutes, in a disabled space. I actually got shouted at by several people, who could yell directly at me, as the top was down. I thought about saying I had an 'unseen disability' but thought better of it and just cowered, pretending not to hear the abuse. Why didn't I move the car, you ask? I'm not sure. I've regretted it ever since. Probably because I couldn't stand the thought of the argument when he came back and found the car *not* there. Life's easier if you go along with his mad ideas, but you just have to live with the consequences.

So, once again, I get out of the car and slink off into the shop as quickly as possible. I should argue with him, I know I should, but sometimes it's just too much effort and … I *am* a mother … with a man-size baby. There's part of me that sort-of agrees with him, if I'm honest. There are so many empty mother and baby/disabled slots … they do seem to have the lion's share. But I'd never say that to him. So … I feel stressed before we've even started.

In this particular mall, you can enter through John Lewis and we meander through the area full of gorgeous household goods, picking up random things. Peter takes my hand and I temporarily forget the parked car, feeling content. Walking hand in hand with a seventy-two year old is weird on one level, but quite sweet, on another. I still can't get my head around it. I love that Jack Nicholson film where one morning, he wakes up and says to himself, 'Who *is* that old woman lying next to me?' I often think about *us* like that: How on *earth* are we suddenly *so* old?

"Shall we have a coffee?" he says, squeezing my hand.

"We've only just got here."

"Yes, I know but it's ..." and he looks at his watch. The time is pretty irrelevant in our lives and particularly irrelevant, when it comes to having a coffee and a slice of cake.

So, we go up the escalators and find our way to the café. There's quite a queue and people are choosing lunch-type things, like soup, sandwiches and burgers, so our break, before we've even started, inevitably turns into lunch. Peter chooses burger and chips.

"Do you really need them already?" I say, like a nagging wife. I feel as if we've only just eaten breakfast, which indeed is true, just an hour and a half ago.

"I need to keep my strength up," he smiles, as if he's

about to go 'over the top' towards the enemy, which in his eyes, he's kind of doing. Anything involved with speaking to strangers, buying something and having to try things on, is like a form of torture.

I choose soup and a roll and have to admit I'm hungry. God knows why, I haven't done much to warrant it. My sole achievement today is that I've actually got out of bed.

We sit next to a young mum and a crying baby. I can't resist it.

"The baby's crying because her mum couldn't find anywhere to park," I whisper, with a grin.

"Very amusing. There were about ten spaces …"

Rather wishing I hadn't brought it up, I move quickly on with, "What sort of shoes are you looking for, then?" (knowing that he's looking for a pair very similar to all his others).

"Not sure till I see them," is his rather enigmatic reply. Peter has been known to buy three pairs of shoes in one go, just because they're good value, comfortable or brown … or a combination of all three and it means he hasn't got to go near a shop again for a decade.

"Shall we split up for a bit?" I say, hopefully.

"Yea, okay. Let's meet in forty-five minutes."

"Where?"

"I don't know … where do you suggest?"

Knowing I want to branch out and visit shops in the main mall, I suggest outside the Apple Store; I always find I'm drawn into it that particular shop, like a magnet. I drift around the beautiful tech devices, like a hungry person in a bakery, looking longingly at the latest iPhone or iPad, wishing I could upgrade.

"Okay, see you there," and without further discussion, he wanders off.

Free to go wherever I want, I head for the main drag and amble in and out of various women's fashion stores. These days, I find I'm at a 'difficult' age. I'm too old for most of the clothes in the shops, but any shops that cater for the 'older woman' make me feel as if I have fast-forwarded into a world of sensible jumpers, tweed skirts, pearls and jolly, practical hats and pretty frocks. I definitely have *not* reached that stage and never will, so what happens is, I end up, every time, back in Marks and Spencers. I go there in the vain hope that there will be something for the older woman that makes me feel young and frivolous. I'm disappointed most of the time and end up buying yet another pair of jeans. When should I stop wearing jeans? Is there an age when jeans are no longer age appropriate?

This time, I go in and browse the myriad styles of jeans (again): jeggings, straight, skinny, boot cut, high rise, low rise, 'boyfriend' (whatever they are) – for God's sake, how is a woman meant to know *what* to choose? Then there's the length – short, medium, long. I pick a black pair (as if I haven't got enough black pairs at home), high rise, straight leg, medium ... they appear to be called *Magic Jeans* which 'support' your stomach, bum and legs *and* hug your waist, apparently ... giving you the contour of supermodel, with 360 degree elasticity (the jeans, not the body). Thinking these do, in fact, sound like a bloody miracle, I enter the changing rooms.

I hate this part, where you strip off and have to stare at yourself from multiple angles, in horrendously bright lights. My old, random bra and pants look particularly unattractive; I feel sorry for my long-suffering husband when I study myself. What a good thing his eyesight isn't what it was. My skin looks saggy, flabby and dimpled and I hear the same old thoughts circulating round my head, of diets, looking like an elephant and being one of the great obese. I close my eyes and hope that when I open them again something might have changed ... but unfortunately, not. The same old body stares back at me with relentless plumpness. I definitely didn't need that lunch ... but then again, does it matter *what* I look like these days? They say women become invisible after hitting fifty. Well, I must have disappeared down a proverbial black hole by now.

Having thoroughly depressed myself with the all round view of my nearly naked body, I pull on the jeans without much hope. But ...they are, for once, a triumph. They do what they say 'on the tin' and I begin to think I'm not so bad for my age. I put my shoes back on and my top and I'm quite pleased with my outline.

I perch on the stool and God, YES, they're very flexible. I can see a tell-tale rim of fat sticking through my top, so I stand up quickly and breathe in. I then have to strip off again and re-dress.

I'm now sweating ... and all thoughts of me looking nice are gone, as I gaze at myself in the goddamn mirrors again. Do I really need yet another pair of black jeans?

I glance at my watch. Ten minutes till I meet Peter. I decide yes, I do *desperately* need them. Anything that can perform magic is an absolute necessity and a bargain. I queue and pay and feel pleased that I've at least got something.

"Hi ..." says Peter, "so you found something? Shoes?"

"No," I murmur. "Jeans."

"You wanted shoes, I thought?"

Oh ... yes I wanted ... shoes.

And *that's* how to go shopping.

Peter is pleased with himself. He's got another pair of brown brogues that look *exactly* like the pair he's got on and several others at home. And he's got another pair of trainers.

"Let's go and have a cup of tea," he says, predictably. "I could do with some cake."

CHAPTER 13

"I married for love but the obvious side benefit of having someone around to find my glasses cannot be ignored." —Cameron Esposito

Us – How Are You? I'm Still Here …

The pair of us have had our fair share of illnesses over the years. And accidents. But we're still here, surprisingly.

Nothing, so far, *life-changing,* thank goodness, but each time, it's made me think of our vulnerability and reliance on each other. As you get older, you realise that you're only one visit away from a doctor, which could radically change your life.

We've both had skin cancer, as mentioned earlier. It's not surprising really, as we've spent a *lot* of our time in the sunshine of Cyprus and visited Australia a few times. Perhaps the surprising part, however, is that out of the two of us, I've got the fair skin, the freckles and the slightly auburn hair and I got the kind of cancer that isn't life threatening and can be removed easily. Peter, though, whose skin goes a wonderful mahogany colour and never burns, got the worst type, that *can* kill you. Mine were squamous and basel cell carcinomas and his was melanoma. Look them up if you don't know the difference. I've had several patches of it: the oddest place was on my finger. Who gets cancer on their finger, for God's sake? (A lot of people apparently, according to the surgeon). I've also had it on my arm, but the worst place was on my face, by the side of my nose, under my eye. I remember lying in a room which you could hardly call an operating theatre; it seemed more like a side-room in the hospital and there were all sorts of people going in and out. There were a lot of conversations going on around me. I lay there, with a piece of cloth over my face; a patch was cut out of it to reveal the place they were going to excise. They were all very nice to me, but I wanted to say, "*Oi, are you taking this as seriously as I am? Can you stop talking about ...*"

I was lying there, worrying about being scarred for life and they appeared to be talking about last night's dinner. Maybe it was a deliberate ploy to make me feel relaxed, but it didn't work. The actual operation wasn't too bad; the worst bit was the injection of anaesthetic around the lesion. I was very tense while he was cutting it out, but I couldn't really feel anything, apart from a little bit of tugging. Afterwards, when I stood up, I felt remarkably weak-kneed and had to sit down for quite a long time. I had a bandage on my face and in my mind's eye, looked like a survivor of some terrible disaster. It healed quickly but there was a long scar on my face that I could have done without. Now, a few years later, you can hardly see it, but every time I'm in the sun, it's a reminder to stay in the shade. I plaster my face with 50 SPF these days, not only to keep cancer away but wrinkles too – but that's a bit stable door-ish. Too little too late. Wrinkles have already set in. Blow all this, *'wrinkles give you character'* and *'wrinkles are where smiles have been'* malarky; give me my young skin back, any day. Mind you, I would never go down the Botox route either. I don't want to end up looking permanently surprised and vacant, in equal measure.

So, to the more serious skin cancer victim. It was sheer luck that it didn't get the chance to kill him. Peter never goes to the doctor, or as rarely as is humanly possible. I can't remember why he'd gone to the doctor in the first place now, but as he was leaving, he'd said to the doctor, 'Could you just look at this thing on my shoulder, please?'

He'd had a strange feeling about this 'thing' for a while and thank God he asked. The doctor didn't like the look of it and acted fast. Fortunately, they got it early and were able to cut it all out but ... there's no real spare flesh on the shoulder and they had to dig deep. The worst bit of the whole procedure was getting a skin graft from his thigh. The doctor had said, helpfully, that it would feel like a 'carpet burn'. They scraped the skin off quite a large area of his leg, leaving a patch that Peter said *'was not like any carpet burn I've ever had'*. It was so painful, he could hardly put his foot down. This skin was then grafted onto his shoulder and to be honest, it looked a ghastly mess. It didn't 'take' well and for a while it didn't look as if it was going to work. Eventually, it did and now there's just a large, shiny scar there.

We've had loads of arguments about using SPF. He refuses, or conveniently forgets to wear any. He might grudgingly put a bit on, if forced to by me, but he would never put it on willingly. Maybe it doesn't feel like a *manly* thing to do? The young men of today are quite happy to use all sorts of products on their skin, but men *of a certain age* just don't want to. Stiff upper lip and all that.

Last year, at the beginning of December, I got Shingles. Now that really *is* a sign of aging, as most people get it when they're old. It seems an appropriate illness to get around Christmas, as it rhymes with *jingles*; it sounds jolly and fun and maybe, even gives you presents? The 'presents' it gives you are lovely blisters on the skin, which are so painful you can't think straight. In my case, annoyingly, they were inside my mouth, which is pretty uncommon. Most *normal* people get them around their waist area but no, not *me*.

I thought I had rampant toothache on a Friday evening, so on Saturday morning, I went to an emergency dentist, who didn't identify it for what it was and sent me home, telling me helpfully to take pain killers. By the Monday morning, when I could see my own dentist, I was overdosing on paracetamol and ibuprofen and considering lopping my head right off. Rather pathetically, I burst into tears in the dentist's chair but when she saw inside my mouth, she was confused but I was telling her that it was toothache and so she arranged for me to come back the next day to have a tooth removed. After another sleepless night, I turned up at the dentist to be told she'd had a re-think and she'd discussed it with colleagues and she was now convinced I had Shingles. The pain was located in one half of my head, stopping in the middle of my chin – classic Shingles, apparently. I'd never given it any thought before, so it came as a shock but at least I'd had a diagnosis that explained everything. For those who are blissfully ignorant of Shingles, it hangs around in your spine after you've had chicken pox, like a malevolent genie and then when your immune system is compromised or you're stressed or old, it pops out and attacks your nerves. Thanks so much, how nice of you to visit.

There's not a whole lot you can do, except wait for the blisters to continue blistering and form a crust and die. I think I was given some special mouthwash and some pills, but nothing helped. I began to take on the look of Joe Bugner with a bad case of acne, had a temperature, couldn't eat and just lay in bed. Peter would pop in now and again but I didn't want to talk to anyone, including him. I had no appetite at all; the only thing I wanted to 'eat' was Knorr Chicken Noodle

Soup. It was like having a pregnancy craving. I hadn't had it for years, but I developed a yearning for it and lived on it for days. My salt levels must have rocketed.

I was like a drug addict, wishing it was time for my next fix. I was alternating between ibuprofen and paracetamol every two hours all through the night and was seriously in danger of overdosing. When the worst of it had gone, I was left with a face that I couldn't bear to touch. Now this sounds okay but I can honestly say, it was one of the worst things I've had to deal with. I gather that all the nerves are left damaged and are trying to heal themselves, which leaves the skin so 'on edge' it would make me feel sick if anything brushed the skin on my face. I went to a pharmacist and consulted Doctor Google many times and I got the depressing news from both, that this can sometimes be how your skin will always feel. God, that was depressing. But … I was one of the lucky ones. For many weeks, my mouth felt odd; my teeth seemed to be disconnected from my gums and cleaning them was a weird sensation, as it was as if they weren't there, but gradually the normal feeling came back. I should think it took six months.

Poor old Peter had to put up with a lot of whinging from me and on the whole he was sympathetic, but he's not the world's best carer. He was happy when I was tucked up in my bedroom, but not so keen on my rather miserable presence downstairs. *I* can't talk, though. I've realised I wouldn't be a great carer, either. It takes a certain type of person to be so *nice* to someone *all* the time. Let's hope neither of us are ever put in that position.

My bout of caring for him came when he fell down the stairs. It was quite a full-on thing to do, just to test my nursing skills and resulted in a certain amount of drama. I'd been out in the room above our garage, which is now a gym/studio. It's been many guises over the years – teenage hangout, disastrous teenage party venue where secreted alcohol was consumed and thrown up; office, photo studio ... but it's now more of an empty space with a few photos in ... and some weights. Yes, weights.

During lockdown, I got into online personal training. I had this gorgeous, funny, fit guy on my laptop screen, telling me 'to do just *five* more' of whatever torture he was putting me through. I must confess I never looked forward to doing it, but when it was over, I felt amazing – very smug that I'd actually done an hour of solid exercise. We had a punch bag hanging from the ceiling and he got me boxing too. Now, *that* I found so satisfying – I could take all my frustrations of Covid, Peter ... *anything* ... out of that dollop of leather. The sessions made me feel vibrant, young and energetic; it was only the next day that my muscles told me otherwise.

I packed up on that particular day and crawled into the house (I might have felt energetic in my head, but my legs were always exhausted) only to find Peter, leaning forward at the bottom of the stairs, unable to breathe.

"What's the matter?" I said, huffily.

"I've fallen down the stairs ..." he groaned.

"Oh my God ... how did you do that?"

"I've got no effing idea. I can't ... breathe ... and ... I've ... hurt ... my ... finger."

There was blood. I'm not very good in emergencies and quite frankly was panicking a bit.

"Can you move?"

"No."

"Shall I phone the doctors?"

"Yes," he mumbled.

I miraculously got through to the surgery and I told them what had happened. I must have been lucky because getting through to a doctor's surgery then (and now) is rather like trying to communicate with the dead. "If he's seventy, I think we ought to see him. I'll get a doctor to ring you back when they can," said the receptionist. So not too much of emergency, then?

We waited for, what felt like, hours and had just decided to go to A and E, when there was a knock on the door. A nice nurse was standing there and said she'd come round to assess the situation. Her assessment was similar to ours, that we should go to A and E, where we were trying to go in the first place.

So we drove the forty minutes to Swindon General to be faced with a dilemma. Do we go to Urgent Care or

Accident and Emergency? He'd had an accident, yes, but it wasn't life threatening, was it? Or maybe it was? Who knew? We went to Urgent Care and he joined about thirty other people who had arrived before him. I was told I wasn't allowed to wait, due to Covid restrictions. Great. So I had to leave him on his own, in a lot of pain, not knowing when he'd be seen.

About four hours later, he rang to say could I go and get him. He *hadn't* been seen by a doctor and hadn't even had an X-Ray, but had just been seen by a nurse. He hadn't broken his ribs but had probably torn all the ligaments around them. I think we could have diagnosed that. To cut a long story short, we're pretty convinced he *had* broken some ribs as months on, he was still feeling the affects, but there was nothing they could have done, apparently. I tried to persuade him to have physio, massages, you name it, I suggested it, but he never did. Peter likes to do things *his* way: to complain a lot; make loud, *old man* noises when he gets out of chairs; never take any pain killers and certainly, never take advice from me.

I suppose that's who he is, but it's quite *annoying*. Understatement of the year.

#

We thought for a long time that the accident had caused a lot of back pain, so, I *finally* persuaded him to go to see a private osteopath; I'd done some research and this guy specialised in sports injuries, played sport himself and I felt maybe Peter would be prepared to see him. I was right and he duly went along to have his back looked at, or manipulated. He'd shown me that if he lay flat on his back with his legs out in front of him, he couldn't flatten one leg. It was weird, you could push his knee down and it was rock solid and if you did flatten it a little bit, his head wanted to come up. It was actually quite funny, in a macabre way. The osteopath took one look at this phenomenon and said, "I think there's something else going on here, mate."

He was right – the *something else* turned out to be wonky hips. Both of them. He got offered six places he could potentially go to see a consultant and we chose one just outside Bath, as theirs was the quickest waiting time. When we googled the hospital, it looked very modern and chic for an NHS hospital, so that confirmed our decision. A hundred percent owned by the NHS, run by private doctors. It wasn't long before he saw the consultant who looked as young as our son, worryingly, but what you have to realise at seventy, is that *everyone* looks young and it's because you're *old*. You wouldn't want someone in their dotage cutting chunks out of your hip, would you?

The consultation revealed both hips were as bad as each other; it was a bit of a toss up which was worse. It was decided to go for the left first and so it was, that only a few weeks later, Peter was offered his op date. We're still somewhat amazed that, despite the year long waiting lists elsewhere, that he just seemed to go to the front of the line.

Hip operations these days are regarded as routine and somewhat mundane. You go in, have your leg cut open, bone chopped around, metal stake inserted, ball and socket joint replaced and Bob's your uncle ... new hip. All under an epidural. Home the same day and then told to get on with it. Do your exercises and you'll be skipping around, in a couple of months. It *does* happen quickly but to me, it doesn't strike me as a particularly easy recovery. Peter's op was at 6 pm and he was out of the hospital by 2 pm the following day.

When I left him there, I felt sick and upset. *He* wasn't – or if he was, he wasn't going to show it.

"Bye then, see you tomorrow."

"Yea, see you. I'll ring later when I'm out," he said. I squeezed his hand and left quickly before my tears came. I drove home and waited nervously for the call. He sounded remarkably okay when he rang and I was able to sleep that night, feeling a little less stressed than I had.

Collecting him, I began to realise that it was a slightly bigger deal than he'd made out. Let's face it, he had a huge gouge out of his leg, a wound about a foot long and bits of ceramic, plastic and metal now living inside him. I felt it was a huge responsibility to be the sole carer. Once we'd got him in the car, the journey home was okay, but then we had to get him up some steps into the house. For thirty years, we'd lived with these steps without railings, but just before the op, we'd managed to get some metal railings fitted and boy, was I pleased we had; just six steps felt like a mountain now. We got him up there and settled in his 'high' chair in the sitting room, where we'd put a single bed. I wasn't keen on him negotiating our spiral staircase, which he'd not that long ago fallen down, but it was soon revealed that he was not comfortable on the single bed and on the second day home, we got him established upstairs. He'd been taught how to go upstairs and was determined to do it.

I became like a fussy old nurse, always telling him to do this, that and the other and he got thoroughly annoyed with me, telling me: *You're not my mother*. Nurse and patient had many stand-offs, shouting matches and silent huffs, but we eventually got through it. I nagged him constantly about doing his exercises:

"Have you done your exercises?"

"YES!"

"How many?"

"You're not my mother." It felt like that notorious dum-dum moment on Eastenders when a character shouted, "You're not my mother!" and the other character shouted back, "Yes, I am!" I certainly felt like the mother of a particularly ungrateful, sullen teenager. I can't wait for the next hip to be done.

#

And so we're five days into the post-op period for the second hip. Peter is now truly bionic with both hips held together with with bits of non-human material and a lot of skill from the surgeon. I wasn't sure whether knowing what was coming was a good thing or not. It was a bit like having a second baby – you conveniently forget the pain, until the contractions actually start and then the sheer agony comes flooding back. I think it wasn't until we were both sitting in the little cubicle, surrounded by white curtains before the op, that we suddenly remembered the reality. I know it wasn't *me* having the op; it was *my* turn to be in the supporting role, as *he* had been with me giving birth – but I felt sick at the thought of the surgeon gouging another hole in his other hip, cutting through bone and shoving alien objects into his leg.

"You may as well go," he said, looking a bit grey around the gills. "There's no point you sitting here for four hours. I'll phone when it's over." I stood up and came over to him and leaning down to kiss him goodbye, I was overcome with a great wave of panic. I didn't show it, but I felt sad. There was my husband of many years, reduced to sitting in an ill-fitting hospital gown with an impenetrable method for doing it up at the back, which involved about six ties; a dressing gown over the top that didn't fit, and blue socks, with white anti-slip patterns on the soles. He was at the mercy of a young surgeon, who breezed in to say *hello* with a mixture of authority, professionalism and cockiness, as he drew a large arrow on his right leg that pointed upwards. It seemed rather rudimentary to say the least; if the arrow had been reversed, would he have done his right knee instead or perhaps lopped his whole leg off?

I said goodbye and left him sitting there alone, scrolling through his phone. Part of me was really glad it was *him* not me, going through it. The thought of someone cutting a twelve inch wound into *my* leg with only an epidural and sedation between me and the knife, was quite frankly, terrifying. The anaesthetist said, he couldn't guarantee that Peter wouldn't be aware of what was happening. As it turned out, both times, he was completely unaware, but the thought of *hearing* sawing and banging was enough for me to want to be completely unconscious, if the same thing ever happened to me. Just cosh me over the head with a large object.

Still, the good thing about this method is that you have none of the side effects of anaesthetic and within minutes of the op being over, he'd been offered something to eat, which he demolished ravenously, as he hadn't eaten anything all day. He rang me and sounded absolutely fine, so I was able to relax at last. I hadn't realised how tense I'd been – but I still didn't sleep and arrived at noon the next day at the hospital, feeling wrung out.

But he'd survived and now it was the period of rehabilitation ... again.

#

We've just driven down the M4 to Bristol yet again for another dental appointment. Our lives are filled with so much fun and frivolity.

Maybe because this last statement isn't exactly true, we are prone to observing 'men at work' on motorways, for want of something more thrilling to talk about. Has anyone else noticed how little work they *actually* appear to do? Today, there was a big sign saying, 'Roadworks Ahead' and then lots of flashing lights and bollards. The traffic all ground to a slow, one line and we crawled for what felt like forever, past the 'roadworks' or lack thereof.

First, we passed a man, hands in pockets, staring morosely into a hole, contemplating his navel or maybe considering throwing himself in it. Then, we crawled past a solitary man carrying a bucket, from where to where, is a mystery. Next, we passed two jovial types having a laugh, as if they were propped up at a bar, telling jokes. Another guy is walking along, looking a bit more promising, but then I realised he was on his mobile, having a nice chat. Maybe he was on the phone to some mystery manager, who was telling him what to do next, but I somehow doubt it. I saw precisely two machines with men doing something constructive. What the hell? I'm sure there's a *plan*, unbeknown to the general public and maybe some men have been working through the night, when we've all been asleep but … the work ethic of the day shift isn't great.

Anyhow ... I digress and let's get back to the stunning subject of Peter's dental appointment. Or appointment*s*. This is just one of many that he's had to attend. Rather like a celebrity, he's having implants, but his aren't visible to the naked eye and don't make him look like Simon Cowell, with ultra bright white tombstones; they are at the back of his mouth and seem to have taken about two years to do. I'd never realised how long you have to wait between work, for the gum to recover; for the bone to grow around the implant; for this, for that. I feel as if we could all be dead by the time they're finished. There will just be a little pile of false teeth left to show that we've walked on this earth.

You may wonder why I have to go with him? Well, the simple answer is, that I don't really, except on the odd occasion when he's had something really horrible done and then I drive home. I've actually grown to like Portishead where his dental clinic is; Mabel and I have trodden our weary way along the brown and murky waters of the Severn Estuary and up the fields rising above it and round the lake, on many an occasion.

I asked Peter why he thinks his teeth are all falling apart and his answer was 'probably all the sugar sandwiches I ate as child'. The almond croissants in Portishead Marina are to die for, by the way. Maybe not such a good snack to eat when your teeth are being replaced, due to the amount of sugar you've consumed in your lifetime. Still, life's too short to worry about such matters.

#

One of the things that defines old age to me is ... going deaf.

If you have to wear glasses, no one bats an eyelid. Glasses can be positively trendy: Prue Leith and Gok Wan make them a fashion statement. Sunglasses make you look cool (or so Peter tells me every day he wears them, when it's grey and dull). But the moment you have to wear a hearing aid, it seems that it gives people the right to make jokes, at your expense. For this reason, I've been rather quiet about recently getting them, something women can do, due to having longer hair styles than men. I haven't even told most people, so anyone who's reading this who knows me well – yes, I have hearing aids. Get over it.

I decided to have my hearing checked about a year ago and discovered I'd lost the 'top part' of my range. It didn't come as a shock, as I was expecting it, but it did make me face up to the fact that I was missing a lot. I'd noticed I 'switched off' in loud company (I sometimes put that down to boredom, which was probably partly true) and I increasingly wanted the subtitles on the TV.

What really got to me was that the audiologist said my hearing had gone equally in *both* ears, so I needed *two* hearing aids. This was doubly aging I thought, decrepit even. He said it was more common to lose hearing in both ears and I asked, clutching at straws, why most people I saw, seemed to wear just one? There didn't seem to be an explanation; he implied that the vast majority of people need two, so I guess it may be just some form of laziness on their part. It is a bit of a faff, to be honest.

It's all very modern and digital nowadays, even with the NHS ones. Your aids can be connected to your mobile phone via bluetooth and be individually 'tuned' to your own particular problems. It was a revelation when he put them on my ears – a strange sensation at first, but once I'd got used to them, it was great. Walking through the countryside, I could suddenly hear the birds twittering in the trees above me; the washing machine warning that the cycle had ended was loud; I could hear the TV.

One of the best things about them is that I can listen to podcasts etc. on my phone without having to put in my Apple iPods. I realise I look a little crazy, however, if someone rings me, as I can speak to them happily and there's no evidence that I'm talking to someone else. Normally, people who walk along talking to themselves are either a) indeed, batshit crazy or b) to be seen wearing headphones etc. So, if I see someone coming, I get my phone out of my pocket to show I'm not a crazy woman. I can also scroll moronically through Instagram videos without annoying everyone else, when in company.

When I heard I was getting them, I made a pre-emptive strike with my children. This was my Whatsapp message to them:

Just so that we get all the jokes out of everyone's system, I now have hearing aids.

Pardon??

Yes yes …. Ha ha!

Actually, they are good and with my hair, you can't see them. I'm much less aware of my tinnitus, which is a big plus. Dad can talk to me from the hall and I can hear him (perhaps not such a big plus). And they are connected by Bluetooth to my phone, so I can answer my phone hands free and listen to music. So, all round I'm glad I've got them.

Also, I'm three times less likely now to get dementia.

So … any jokes anyone??

It's half past two ….. love, Mum xx

To be fair to them, they haven't made many jokes since then. I don't wear them every day (as I said, sometimes I can't be bothered with the faff) but I'm used to them now and can forget I've got them in. I often say to Peter he could do with being checked out, but so far, I haven't persuaded him to go. His hips and teeth are enough to be going on with. You do have to be pretty dextrous to change these teeny, tiny batteries; with Peter's arthritic thumbs, he'd have great fun trying to manipulate them out of their housing. Old age is fun, isn't it?

That's another little job for me, I think, when the time comes.

CHAPTER 14

"Because I always say, if you're married for 50 years, and 10 of them are horrible, you're doing really good!" —Michelle Obama

If Music Be The Food Of Love – Maybe Don't Play On

I've mentioned, on many occasions, how different we are, and music is an area of our lives which clearly demonstrates this. I like it and he doesn't.

When I say I like it, I mean I *love* it and when I say he doesn't, I mean he's totally *disinterested*. Music has passed him by; it's floated around him like an early morning mist, lightly touched him, but evaporated without trace. Whereas for me, it's in my soul; I'd hate life without it.

We've been to loads of concerts and festivals during our time together, but I know he's only doing it for me, which is kind of him, under the circumstances. Given a choice, he would never waste his time in that way; he'd so much rather go to a sporting event. To an outsider, he looks as if he's acting like anyone else: moving to the rhythm, singing along and clapping his hands, but I know he's going through the motions. I suppose it's like *me* pretending to be interested in Lewis Hamilton's latest win.

"Hamilton's just taken the lead … only five laps to go," he might say.

"Wow, amazing," I say, not meaning it at all; thinking to myself, I can hardly contain my effing excitement. To be fair to me, I have gone to watch sport with him, Wimbledon mainly. I think I'd just annoy him if I went to watch rugby with him as I blatantly don't understand the rules.

But that's what marriage is about, isn't it? It's continuously having to adapt to someone else's preferences. I suppose life would be pretty boring if we both liked the same things or we did the same job. Imagine the conversations over the breakfast table, if we'd both been teachers … or flew planes? We'd have been talking about the latest developments in education or flying technology, in between munching on our toast. Horrendous.

When I say I love music, I don't love *all* music. I'm very much a modern music fan; classical, opera and jazz leave me a bit cold. Well, completely cold, if I'm honest. What a heathen, some of you intellectuals are no doubt thinking, but that's me: university educated, with a decidedly unsophisticated taste in most things.

Pop over classical; musicals over Shakespeare; easy-read novels over academic ones; soap operas over serious drama; police crime series over spy films ... the list of things that I've wasted my education on, is endless.

I like to feel I've got an eclectic taste in pop music, though. Whenever I listen to Desert Island Discs (which I do whenever I can) I ponder which eight discs I'd take to the island and I usually can't get past the first one because the choice is too difficult. Bands/musicians that have had an impact on my life are numerous. For starters, perhaps: The Beatles, Stevie Wonder, Nat King Cole, George Michael, Whitney Houston, Fleetwood Mac, Harry Styles and Coldplay. But you've then got to pick ONE song ... *Hey Jude ... You are the sunshine of my life ... Unforgettable ... Freedom ... I will always love you ... The Chain ... As it Was ... Yellow.* But that doesn't seem remotely adequate. 'Can I have the whole of Coldplay as my luxury item, please Lauren?'

'No, that's not part of the rules'. And so the uncertainty begins – what about: *I'm not in Love* by 10cc? Or Queen's *Bohemian Rhapsody*? James Blake's *Assume Form*? Sam Smith's *Too Good at Goodbyes*? *Finally* by CeCe Peniston? And don't get me started on Taylor Swift ... but more of her, later. I could go on and on and ON, but I won't. This is the sort of thing that Peter would find impenetrable and frankly, *utterly* boring. He wouldn't know who half the above people *are,* never mind know the songs. Same as

I find his ability to answer, correctly, the name of the tennis player who beat some other famous tennis player at some famous venue in 1968, utterly astounding. On this basis, we do, in fact, make great Pub Quiz partners. I can answer music, literature and entertainment questions and he can answer sport, geography and history. You see … we make a good team.

Our most recent visit to a music event was a strange one. I'd been complaining that we never went anywhere in the evenings, rather unfairly, to be honest. I used to enjoy going out a lot, but I've noticed we both prefer to stay in, watch TV most nights and go to bed early. If we do venture out, we consider 11.30 really late now. I used to be a night bird, but not any more. I'm early to bed and late to get up, now.

I saw that there was a worldwide showing of a *live* Coldplay concert coming from Buenos Aires, in all cinemas. I know by my age, I should be beyond this … but I'm not. You've probably gathered that I'm just a *bit* of a Coldplay fan. I asked Peter if he would accompany me and expecting him to say he'd rather stick needles in his eyes, he actually said *yes*. I thought he would fall asleep by about the second note, but to give him his credit, he stayed awake the entire time and said, "I actually quite enjoyed that," when it was over. Praise indeed … and I really appreciated him going with me. Seeing the sheer size of the stadium on a huge screen and having spectacular drone footage, enhanced the experience. The digital wristbands that make patterns in the crowd, the fireworks, the huge screens, the sheer enthusiastic joy of the crowd, made me *wish* I was in Buenos Aires, but this was a pretty good second. I'd been worried that we'd stick out like a sore thumb in the cinema audience but they were an assorted bunch – people our age, families with children and everyone in between. We weren't a very noisy crowd; some people wanted to cheer and clap at the end of each song, but we were mostly rather reticent; it seemed very *un-British* to make a noise in a cinema auditorium.

I'd only been to one actual 'live' concert of Coldplay in the past and it was before they'd become the huge mega-band they are today. I've been a fan since the very beginning and followed their journey from *popular* in 2000 with the release of 'Yellow', through to *very popular* all through the noughties, to everyone wanting to be seen to *hate* them after that – and *finally* ... through to their current global mega tours, to hundreds of thousands of adoring fans.

The concert I went to was at the Royal Albert Hall. My eldest daughter worked at the Roundhouse and had met the band several times. She knew I was a big fan and one day rang me from work. This was unusual and when she asked me casually, "Are you doing anything today?" I wondered why she was asking.

I said, "No, nothing."

She replied, with a giggle, "Would you like to come to a Coldplay concert with me tonight?"

Well, you've never seen anyone move quicker. There was only one ticket, so Peter wasn't even considered, I'm afraid. He dutifully took me to the station and wished me a good time. I can remember sitting on the train to Paddington, in a dream. This was a chance in a lifetime for me and I didn't even have to pay for the ticket.

We were only about twenty rows back from the band. The Albert Hall is actually small compared to the venues they play now and maybe I didn't realise at the time quite how privileged I was. We were both hyper-excited and sang along and waved our hands, the whole time. I realised I knew every word of every song and it felt as if Chris was singing it all for me. The fact that every other person in the concert felt exactly the same, was irrelevant. I loved every minute of it.

After the end, my daughter asked, "Would you like to come to the after-party with the band?" Well, I was virtually beside myself … and we both made our way to the venue as fast as our legs could carry us. The band didn't arrive for a while; I kept looking at the door in anticipation. We were at the bar when my daughter said, "Don't turn round now, Mum, but they've just walked in."

I felt like a love-sick teenager: nervous, sweaty palms, heart palpitations. I realised I had absolutely *nothing* to say to Chris that would *not* make me look like a total pillock. What *do* you say to someone you've worshipped from afar, for so long? I *could* have spoken to him; I could have gone and introduced myself, I was *that* near and it was *that* possible ... but all I could think of to say was, "*I love your music,*" and I really didn't think Chris would be *that* interested. He was probably tired after the concert, anyway and the last thing he'd want was to be hassled by some demented woman. So I avoided them for the rest of the evening, trying to look casual, but watching them from a distance. Even as I write this, (I'm so pathetic) I think, *Oh maybe, one day, Chris will read this and invite me to a concert.*

God, I'm sad.

I look back now and regret that I didn't at least say 'Hi'.

#

Reading books isn't quite the same as music with us both –we both read a lot, but completely different things. I read what can only be described as 'women's fiction' and he reads 'adventure' 'spy' and 'historical' – in other words, anything I don't read. It's strange that there is a genre called *Women's Fiction* – rather a derogatory name, I think – pronounced *wimin,* in the manner of someone referring to the weaker sex: *Wimin, know your place.* Why don't they lump together what men like to read and call it *Men's Fiction*? It somehow wouldn't have the same demeaning feel, though, would it? I can only read novels firmly placed in 'real' life: stories about relationships, families, love and conflict. Women's Fiction is defined by saying it's usually about the protagonist's (usually female) emotional journey. Don't men have emotional journeys? Ha ha, maybe that's the difference.

The stories I read will also only be set in modern times; very rarely will they be set in the past. I don't know why I only read these, it's not that I've set out to restrict myself to a certain genre, but I'm simply not interested in other types of fiction. I could no more read a book about spies, vampires or alien planets, than do a Maths degree. I've spent a lot of my time now writing said genre too. Still, it's good to '*write what you know*'.

Having studied English Literature, I put my easy-read-only-reading-matter down to having had my *fill* of historical, literary and *erudite* books back in the seventies. Endless Shakespeare, Chaucer and even Beowülf, in the original Anglo-Saxon, was my area of expertise at university, along with impenetrable Victorian poetry and hugely long novels, like 'Middlemarch'. After coming to my senses and realising I *didn't* want to do a Phd, I put all those books I'd studied on shelves, never to be opened again. They lived in my bookcases for many years and I was reluctant, for some reason, to get rid of them, but recently I've been de-cluttering and I'm afraid all those academic books have finally been laid to rest. Ever since seeing three different Shakespeare plays on three consecutive nights at university (Birmingham University had strong links with Stratford) I've hardly *ever* sat for three hours, struggling through the language of Shakespeare again. Relatively recently, I *did* see one of his plays at Curium Amphitheatre in Cyprus. The location was spectacular, with the Mediterranean spread out beyond the stage and the sun gently setting, but I *still* didn't enjoy it. Most of the audience were Russians and there was a teenager sitting in front of me, who blatantly didn't understand one word of the play. I had quite a fellow feeling with him and a certain amount of sympathy.

It really did sound like a foreign language to me, too.

CHAPTER 15

"Some people ask the secret of our long marriage. We take time to go to a restaurant two times a week. A little candlelight, dinner, soft music, and dancing. She goes Tuesdays, I go Fridays." —Henny Youngman

Us During The Pandemic 2020 – 2022

The pandemic was a strange time for everyone, wasn't it? We were all bumbling along, minding our own business and then …we were hurled into the biggest global event any of us had ever seen. Now that it's over, it's hard to remember exactly what happened and when, but in a way, it doesn't matter. I think we all look back on it now, if we survived relatively unscathed, as a time that is best forgotten.

I know that we were incredibly lucky. We didn't live at the top of a high-rise with young children. We didn't have jobs that we were trying to do at home. We didn't have old relatives stuck in care homes. We didn't have school-age children having to be taught at home, on Zoom. We weren't living on our own and dying of loneliness. We had each other; we lived in the country, in a nice house with a garden; our kids were all okay. We, unlike many, can actually look back and say, 'It wasn't too bad, really.'

I was scared, at first, like everyone else. None of us knew what was going to happen and I imagined the worst. I can remember holding my breath, when I walked past people (even though we were socially distanced). I remember *not* touching stiles and field gates when out walking, in case they were contaminated. I can remember seriously considering washing our shopping (but thank goodness I saw sense). I remember watching the news constantly, frightening myself stupid.

But I also remember the wonderful weather in the spring of 2020. Our son escaped London, just before the first lockdown and the three of us spent days exploring walks that we'd never done before, wandering in the sunshine across beautiful landscapes, feeling a million miles away from the global worry. We didn't see a soul and the feeling of being outside and in the sun, was magical and healing.

The day our son arrived from London was funny, now I look back. We were so worried about catching the virus back then, that we all agreed that he could come home, as long as he isolated for about five days. I kitted out his room with tea and coffee and snacks and brought him meals, which I left outside his door. He was very good about it and our house was big enough for us to avoid contact, but how crazy was that? I'm surprised I didn't give him a bell to ring ... *unclean, unclean.*

He can effectively work anywhere, so he just carried on working as usual, but Peter and I had to find things to occupy ourselves. If I'm honest, it felt pretty normal for us – we were just doing what we always do: walking, gardening, reading, watching TV. Peter had even more time to shout at unsuspecting call centre workers and spent a lot of time sorting his 'paperwork'. The call centre workers were now working from home, so after a heated call with Peter, they could go and make themselves a nice cup of tea, before facing another customer.

Everyone else seemed to be learning how to cook sourdough or how to knit, so I took it upon myself to learn how to play the piano. My mother had left me a bit of money and with it, I bought a piano, hoping that, at some point, one of us would attempt to learn how to play it. Peter was never going to learn, the children played it and one of them got to Grade 5 – but I never did, so it seemed like the right time to try. With the help of some online teaching aids, I attempted to learn scales and basic tunes. It was rudimentary to say the least, but my fingers *did* begin to move more easily and I began to understand the notes, a *little* bit. I spent hours doing this, secretly disappointed that I didn't sound like Chopin or at least, Elton. I've been told that I have the sort of personality that wants to do things *immediately* and finds it frustrating when I don't know how to do something; this trait was certainly demonstrated with my attempt to learn music. It's so complicated trying to coordinate your fingers, your brain, your feet and your hearing. I realised that learning the piano at my age was nigh on impossible. I'm not making any excuses but ... I eventually got bored and one day I shut the lid and never opened it again. If I opened it today, I don't think I'd remember *one* thing.

The other activity I did was to employ an online personal trainer, as I mentioned before. I found this excellent (apart from the internet often being annoying). I can't say I looked forward to it but when I was actually doing it, I loved it. It was an hour of intense exercise, which I'd never have done without him. Even through the screen, he was able to motivate me to do 'one more' of whatever excruciating movement I was doing. I was always relieved when it was time to lie down on the mat – it wasn't for relaxing, but for yet more exercises in the lying position, but it felt like the easier option.

The other thing I did was something I would have only got round to, under these circumstances. I had literally hundreds of photos that I'd inherited from my mum. I spent hours chucking out landscapes I had no idea about, but writing on the back of photos of friends and relatives, so that in the future, someone would know who the photo was of. My logic was that when I die, my children won't have a clue who these people are, so it was my job to at least *try* to show them their lineage.

It was remarkably satisfying and I ended up putting it all together in a book, to hand on to them. It made sense of *my* past too and I wished I'd asked my mother more questions, but you never think you're going to need to know, do you? It's only when someone's gone that you realise how little you *knew* about their lives. Looking through all her stuff, I realised how different her life could have been, if her first love hadn't gone down in a submarine during the war. She wouldn't have had to marry my awful dad, but then I wouldn't have existed, I suppose. She too had been alive during the other pandemic, but was only a baby. It struck me how sad it is that her life is now reduced to a book of old photos, but I suppose one day, mine will be as well. It makes me realise how precious life is. The pandemic certainly made life more precarious and emphasised the fragility of everything. It's a shame that humans can't seem to appreciate the 'every day' until something happens to jolt them out of their torpor.

At any time during the period of the pandemic when restrictions were lifted in some way, Peter and I took advantage of 'getting out'. A lot of people our age didn't go anywhere, but we took the attitude that we haven't got that much time left and we didn't want the pandemic to ruin our lives. So, we went to Cornwall a couple of times and even flew to Cyprus, when we were allowed to. I remember arriving at Paphos with my digital Covid pass, wondering if we'd be allowed in and what would happen, if we weren't. We were met on the tarmac by people checking our passes and the woman I got, had no idea how to read them and *I* had to show *her*. We were eventually ushered through, with no problem at all. I don't think we'd have gone if we'd been staying in a hotel, but our house is on a cliff in splendid isolation, so we were able to hang out up there, without seeing anyone. The only difference to England was that you had to show your pass in the supermarket, which seemed like a good idea to me.

The other thing I did during the pandemic was ... I bought a dog. I know – everyone was doing it and it led to a hike in prices and to more dogs being abandoned when it was all over, but I knew I wanted a dog forever, not just for Covid. My beautiful, previous Labrador had been dead for six months and I missed having a dog's presence in the house, but I'd grieved for Juno as if she was a person and it didn't seem right just to *replace* her. But when the pandemic struck, it somehow was the right time and I became obsessed with looking at rescues on the internet. I soon came to my senses when I realised that rescues come with a lot of baggage and I decided to buy a puppy instead.

I did *literally* everything wrong: I found Mabel on the internet and I never met her mother or father (until after the pandemic was over). I only saw her on video and only met her owner on Whatsapp and paid the money over, before physically seeing her. In theory, it was bonkers but you know when you have a 'feeling' about something and it turns out your 'feeling' was *right*? That's what happened. Her owner and I 'clicked' – she was a lady of my age and her dog was just her pet, not a breeding machine. She wanted future owners of her puppies to be people who weren't going to 'go back to the office' after the pandemic and I think she could tell, even on the computer, that I wasn't one of those.

She lived in North Wales, so to add even more of a dodgy scenario to the story, Mabel's owner's daughter happened to be coming our way and we arranged to meet in a motorway stopover. As she handed over this little scrap of black fur to me outside Greggs, it felt as if we doing some kind of drug deal. I almost expected the Covid police to jump out and arrest us. She was as good as gold in the car home and she's been as good as gold, ever since.

She gave us a *reason* to walk the hundreds of miles we did during those strange years.

CHAPTER 16

Being someone's first love may be great, but to be their last is beyond perfect." —Anonymous

Us On The Mean Streets Of London ... And Christmas At Home, December 2023

Today is a beautiful autumnal day in November, 2023. I've just taken Mabel out for a walk with a new harness on, which impressed me, but not her. She objects to harnesses, as she feels she's too good to wear one, but what she doesn't realise is that she's super strong and can pull me over, at will. She wears it under sufferance and gives me filthy looks, while it's being done up.

The sun's shining through golden leaves and low and behold, the sky is blue. The weather has been non-stop rain for weeks and everywhere around here is knee-high in mud, which for once, isn't an exaggeration. You take your life in your hands on one of my favourite walks down to the river – it's so slippery you're in danger of sliding straight into the water, if you make it that far. I've banned Peter from walking that way since his hip op, as I don't want a hip dislocation added to his many medical issues of the day.

This is a slightly strange preamble into this chapter. I wanted to write about the *other* side of our life which I haven't as yet talked about, away from the countryside. It struck me last week on a train to London. We were sitting, silently reading our Kindles and mobile phones, occasionally glancing out at the passing scenery and worrying about whether the 'trolley' was going to come our way, so we could buy the inevitable 'coffee and cake' while whizzing along. Any person on the train who could be bothered to give us any of their attention, would see a very boring couple: him, with a good head of grey hair, wearing a kind of country wax jacket that didn't exactly look like slick, London garb (and is not the traditional country wax jacket either; a sort of *hybrid,* produced by M and S which they think can straddle both lifestyles) and her, with a camel coat and paisley scarf, long boots and hair that is *sort of* blond; she's trying to look smart, but doesn't quite pull it off. They don't speak to each other much, apart from "Coffee or tea?" when the trolley does, eventually, come their way, much to their relief.

So what *on earth* are these two doing on a train to London, you might ask? Well, as I walked next to Peter down the platform towards the Elizabeth Line,

I said to him, with a giggle, "I wonder how many other people on the train are going to a photographic exhibition of naked, ginger men?"

"Not many, I would think," he said with a grin. "Quite a niche ..."

Let me explain. Our son, took it upon himself ten years ago to start trying to make ginger men desirable and sexy; at the time, there were no ginger models and only a handful of ginger, leading men and they were usually in the role of the *nerd*, the *angry one* or the downright *weird* one. So, he started taking portraits of handsome gingers and published a book. The whole idea hit a nerve and he ended up taking his exhibition all over the world and getting lots of press. Many people thought it was just going to be a one-hit wonder, but ten years later, he's heading towards the 200,000 Instagram followers mark and runs a successful company, with calendars, clothing, digital products and books, dedicated to redheads.

So this was why we were going to London – to attend the launch of his third book, a rather more daring photo collection, this time of *naked* gingers. As he says, *Give the punters what they want* – and he's certainly been proven right, as he's already sold thousands of books. As he pointed out in his speech, we've attended just about everything he's put on and travelled abroad to do it: to New York, Sydney and Rotterdam. This time, we made our way to Soho, London and entered the world of beautiful, ginger men. We were, without doubt, the oldest attendees, but there were a few who weren't far off our age. Mostly though, they were young, attractive thirty-somethings, of all genders and races. Many of the guests were red-haired, so it was a fitting autumnal gathering.

There's nothing like going to a trendy Soho venue, full of young, beautiful people and loud music with a DJ, to make you feel *ancient* and as if life is passing you by. We're often in bed by ten at home, but in London at ten o'clock, the night has only just started and you begin to realise that other people have a LIFE. Everyone's out on the streets at ten, nursing pints of beer or wine glasses, as the pubs are full to bursting point. Queues are outside clubs. Tuk-Tuks, with deafeningly loud dance music blaring and bright lights flashing, are being peddled noisily down streets. Restaurants are full to the brim with people. Crowds are on pavements. Double-decker buses, steamed up, are pushing their way through pulsating traffic and all on a Wednesday night, not even a Friday or Saturday. It makes you realise that you're *definitely* not young any more, as you begin to dream of your electric-blanket-warmed bed and a nice cup of cocoa.

But ... I love it. It's so lovely to feel part of this exciting life, this *energy* and ambition. I believe *all* seventy year olds should go to naked ginger exhibitions, just to keep them on their toes and not fall into miserable old age.

Our son has definitely kept us young in other ways. I remember another time, years ago now, we were going to Soho, this time, to watch him sing in his band. We were late and I asked a passer-by, "Are we going the right way to Madame Jo-Jo's?"

The guy looked a bit askance and said, "Yes ... but you *do* know what it is, do you?"

And yes, we *did* know – the iconic Raymond's Review Bar turned Gay club. He must have seen us and wondered what on earth we were doing going there, but we went to see our son play in lots of different venues and went with him to lots of gay bars too. I always liked it – they felt so unthreatening as a woman and so welcoming. Peter was fine about it too and so we 'gaily' went around, visiting all sorts of places. Recently, he had another exhibition, showcasing portraits from fifty years of Pride. It embraced all queer culture and again we went and loved the talks, the music and, of course, the photos. I told him the only thing I couldn't get to grips with was the word '*queer*' – as it used to be so offensive *in our day*, but is now embraced by the gay community. Just another example of how you've got to *keep up* or get left behind.

I also went to a 'trans' conference a few years ago, *way* before 'trans' became such a difficult and toxic issue to talk about. It was so interesting and ever since then, I've read as much as I can about trans people and their rights.

So ... next time you're on a train and you see a couple who look as though they're going for gentle shop in Oxford Street ... they might be going somewhere completely different. I remember one of my bosses once said to me, *Never Assume* ... I didn't think much about it at the time, but now it makes sense.

#

It's December 2023 and just a couple of weeks to go until Christmas. It's that crazy time of year when for some reason we've all forgotten, we put an unsuspecting tree in our house, put garish, plastic things on it and reams of lights that twinkle, somewhat annoyingly. Or, in our case this year, flash in a manic way, alternating different colours, because I can't find the setting where they just *stay on*. I wasn't even going to put a tree up this year, as my heart wasn't in it. Let me explain.

Christmas here, in our family house, has always been *full* of people – and I mean, full. Last year, there were sixteen of us and it was my ultimate responsibility to make sure everyone had *a wonderful Christmas time* (cue, jolly music). Not every year has been like that, some years it was maybe eight or ten, but the point is, it's always been a big, family Christmas.

Since the children were little, we've always made sure our house is decorated to excess. It kind of lends itself, with its central spiral staircase, upon which you can wind hundreds of lights. The house has a big hall where you can place the tree, so it lights up the whole house. When you pull up in a car outside, you can see the 'stairway to heaven' effect and the tree, through the window.

Every year, the ceremonial getting down of the tree, baubles and tinsel out of the attic has filled me with a certain amount of dread, but once I get going, I've enjoyed the ritual: the bickering, as Peter and I unwind the lights unsuccessfully and end up with a tangled mess; the very serious discussions about whether to start the lights from the top or the bottom of the tree; me, saying to him, *Do we really need so many lights this year?* (every year) as he places yet another set round some curtains, another round a window and even outside, around the front door; the inevitable breakages of special baubles dating back to the middle ages, before the birth of plastic; the pine needles *literally* everywhere, despite the fact that it's an artificial tree (how does *that* work?) and the little bits of silver plastic that seem to get everywhere.

Every year, I've suggested we buy a *real* tree; we bought our current one a lifetime ago, in Cyprus, in the nineties. It was the only alternative as there weren't any good, *real* trees out there then and to be fair, this one is a pretty good artificial one. I never dreamt we'd still be putting it up in 2023, thirty years later, but here we are ... and it's still dropping needles; you'd think there wouldn't be any left by now. It's overseen thirty years of festivities: been covered in bags of chocolate money, been festooned with 'tree presents' (a family tradition), had huge piles of presents under it and watched over, as the children excitedly transferred them into the sitting room after lunch, making individual piles, next to sofas and chairs. We were of the opinion that main presents had to be opened after lunch, so we could all spend the day *anticipating.* This is where stocking and tree presents would come in handy – these distracted the kids until the orgy of opening, which was usually after a long lunch, at about four o'clock, when the whole room ended up like a festive jumble sale, full of paper. The tree has overseen the children playing with new toys; the adults kissing each other and thanking each other for gifts they didn't really want and the dog, rolling around in the discarded paper, squashing presents and playing with her new ball that Santa gave her. It's funny the little traditions that families acquire – this was how we did it when I was a child and I passed it on.

So … to get back to *this* year. The whole thing feels like an excuse for commercial excess to me … but I'm grumpy, as no one's coming to us this time. To make an effort to decorate the house, just for Peter and me, feels utterly pointless. If it had been up to me, I wouldn't have even put up the tree, but Peter insisted. Which is weird, as every year it's *me* who sends all the Christmas cards, buys the presents and cooks the turkey. All *he* has to do is turn up and wear a silly hat out of a cracker … but the decorations have always been his domain, I suppose and perhaps he doesn't want to let go.

Christmas without children is horrible, I've decided.

Without their innocent belief in Father Christmas and their excitement over new toys, what's left? Advertisements on the telly starting in early November; extortionate postage costs and long queues at post offices; supermarkets full of Christmas tat; cookery programmes giving you advice on how to have a stress-free Christmas Day (*what?*) and horrible, tinny Christmas songs playing in shops, lifts, pubs and any other venue possible.

I'm definitely becoming a cynical old bat.

#

We've just come back from a few days in London; a birthday treat for Peter and a chance to see some of the sites and culture. To say we're exhausted is putting it mildly – last night, I could hardly drag my feet back to the flat we were staying in. We took full advantage of everything the metropolis had to offer and as it's nearly Christmas, there were added lights.

When did London change so drastically from a litter-strewn, generally dirty sh*t hole, to a place so filled with high-rise, glass monuments to money, that it feels as if the whole city is being re-built? Wherever you look, there are enormous cranes, silhouetted against the sky.

Take Tottenham Court Road station exit. You come out into somewhere that feels more like China or America: huge screens (and I mean, *huge*) with something called *The Outernet* – digital art all around you, in hyper-colour. Think … the old Piccadilly

Circus, on steroids. It's now the most visited London attraction. Then travel on the new Elizabeth Line – a haven of clean, wide platforms, where trains draw in behind closed doors, to stop people throwing themselves in front of them ... and carriages that move smoothly, don't rattle and are positively comfortable to travel in. You walk out and up the steepest escalators, walls unadorned by graffiti, into a new world.

Soho is now full of million pound flats with no one living in them, posh galleries and coffee shops, every two meters. Gone are the dubious clubs, the dodgy dives of yesteryear. This was the London we saw this time. We walked for miles on our first day, through thousands of tourists, on our way through Seven Dials, through theatre land (tickets from £195 – *are you joking?*) down to Trafalgar Square, to mingle with throngs of people meandering through the Christmas markets, listening to carol singers and then into the National Portrait Gallery, for a mooch around (free of charge) to see such treasures as Van Gogh's Sunflowers, Caravaggio masterpieces and Stubbs' horses. Back through China Town, down onto the tube, to fall into bed exhausted.

Second day – very cultured and sacred, with visits to St Bartholomew's the Great and St Paul's Cathedral. Although neither of us are religious, for some reason, we enjoy looking round churches. Peter, particularly, will spend ages reading plaques about people we've never heard of. I find I have a limit; for some reason, standing looking at things in museums and churches is unbearably tiring and I eventually slope off to find somewhere to sit.

Third day: a walk to the British Museum (a bit of a misnomer, in my humble opinion). The whole museum seems dedicated to the foreign treasures we've plundered. How many artefacts have we 'acquired' over the centuries? I know some of them would have been destroyed if we hadn't rescued them, but honestly, I *do* think we should give some of them back. I had no idea how enormous the Elgin Marbles' collection was. I just wonder how we'd feel if some foreign country had nicked our treasures. But … who am I to judge?

Kings Cross is another area of London that has been totally transformed: from a bombed out area, to a playground of dancing fountains, twinkling trees and large screens. There are masses of shops and an old, round gas storage facility transmogrified into million pound accommodation for the mega-rich and just a little further on, glass cathedrals to the genius of Google. While visiting, we went on a digital trip to the moon, courtesy of Tom Hanks, at the Lightroom in Coal Drops Yard. A fantastic experience – surrounded by screens that made you feel as if you were on the moon, with the astronauts.

So, all in all, we had a fantastic experience and again it was obvious to me that we lead a very sheltered life back in Wiltshire. The only parts of the trip that weren't pleasant were the train journeys to and fro.

For once, the trains were on time, in both directions, but they say *'hell is other people'* ... and my God, they're right. Both ways, we had the misfortune to sit near people who seemed to regard the train carriage as an extension of their living room, continuing their conversations at high volume as they would at home, moving about the carriage for no reason and eating copious amounts of snacks. On both journeys, I was on the 'outside' and was the nearest to the other people shouting; Peter pretended he wasn't there and just glared occasionally. I had to put up with being banged on the shoulder several times, the megaphone voice of the man of the family talking inanely almost directly into my left ear and the disgusting smells of the spicy food being consumed.

Apart from that, the journey was fantastic.

CHAPTER 17

"After a while, you just want to be with the one that makes you laugh." —Chris Noth as Mr. Big, Sex and the City

I Left My Heart In San Francisco

And so, one bleak February Saturday morning, I ventured out into the world, alone.

No, I wasn't going up Ben Nevis or trekking across the Sahara ... or swimming the Channel ... or anything remotely adventurous. I was flying to San Francisco, on my tod. This isn't ground-breaking, I know, but after decades of doing everything together, to go on such a long trip without my partner in crime, seemed like a huge deal to me. Now I'm back, it feels simply like an old lady's trip away, but the build-up in my mind was tumultuous. It's not as if I haven't done it before. I went there on my own a few years back, but that was pre-pandemic and the world and I have changed since then.

First of all, let me explain why I went ... my oldest daughter and her husband now live there. She has three children and it's a huge expense for her to come this way and I miss them all, every day. But why did I go on my own? Peter was still recovering from his second hip operation. He'd got over the first few weeks and was now staggering around with a certain amount of ease, but he wasn't allowed to fly long-haul. I had been getting depressed at never seeing the 'Californian contingent' as I call them and he said one day, "Why don't you go over there, then?", as if it was something you could just 'do' without any thought. To him, hopping on a plane was part of his job and didn't involve the kind of soul-searching I'm capable of. Not the *'Save The Planet'* type of soul-searching, I must confess, but the *'Will I die?'* type.

I'm not a good flyer, as you can probably surmise. If you saw me, seemingly casually reading a book during take-off, you'd think I was a seasoned traveller, who doesn't give a toss about being flung heavenwards in a tin can, to thousands of feet above the ground. I do my level best to pretend to *myself* and the rest of the world, that I'm absolutely FINE with the process. But ... every time I take that final step onto the plane, I'm *actually* saying to myself, "Well, this is it. My last contact with mother earth."

I can almost hear Peter saying, *'For God's Sake ...'*

I can be told endlessly that it's statistically safer than travelling down the motorway, but my brain isn't convinced. How can something as big as an A380 possibly lift itself into the air? Perhaps if I understood the mechanics of flight it might help, but somehow, I don't think so. I have to admit, I've been in loads of planes and survived all of *those* journeys, surprisingly, so I'm not sure why I think the *next* one, will be *the one*.

When I met Peter, I hadn't really been anywhere, but his family were professional travellers; his father was a 617 squadron pilot in the war and B.O.A.C pilot afterwards and they'd always flown to exotic places all over the world. I went with Peter, his parents and brother to the Canaries soon after I met them all; to them, it was just another trip abroad, but to *me*, it was the most exciting thing I'd done so far in my little life. I was amazed to see bananas growing … that's how insular I was. I remember Peter saying that he'd never sat next to someone on a plane who looked so unutterably *terrified* before. I broke out in a cold sweat, I was ashen white and visibly trembled whenever the plane made a different noise or vibrated. His whole family found it all very amusing and I can still hear his mother saying, "There's not much point being nervous. If we're going to crash, there's nothing you can do about it, so you may as well relax".

Great advice … thanks for that.

I'm not such a gibbering wreck now; by sheer familiarity, I can *sort of* relax, as long as I can convince myself that I'm, in fact, somewhere else. I watch films with a manic focus; the moment one's finished, I'm onto the next, so that my brain doesn't have time to realise where it is. Strangely, I don't mind take-off or landing; it's the turbulence I hate. Even now, I break into the sweats and my heart pounds – a physical reaction to something that feels 'wrong' to me. I heard yesterday that due to climate change, turbulence is getting worse. I can't wait for my next trip.

So ... yes, I *really* wanted to see my daughter and family, but did I want to put myself through all this? I didn't tell Peter, but I changed my mind a million times, from ... *Absolutely, yes, of course I want to go,* to ... *No, I don't want to die.* He would have found my vacillations tedious and unfathomable, so I kept them to myself.

Once I'd decided to get a grip and not be so pathetic, I booked the ticket and felt relieved that I'd finally seen sense. It was as if I'd given myself permission, somehow, to go ... and I felt like a weight had been lifted from my shoulders. I did, however, ruin the cheap flights I'd found, by worrying about where to sit on the plane; again, not something that would cross Peter's mind. I ended up spending nearly £80 extra, so that I could be on an aisle seat, as near to the front of the plane as possible – in pursuit of less turbulence and the ability to get out and skip to the loo, whenever I wanted to. Peter seems to have the bladder capacity of a elephant, so doesn't care where he sits, but I like to go at least twelve times on any flight. The thought of being 'stuck' for eleven hours by some large, snoring bloke, quite frankly appalled me; the only way to move would be to wake the monster up or climb over him in an undignified way. Eleven hours can be a very long time to be pinned to a seat, desperate for a wee.

The day arrived and Peter took me to a National Coach stop. He'd offered to drive me to Heathrow, but I wasn't sure he should be driving at all with his new hip, never mind driving all that way, so we opted for a compromise – the romantic setting of Cirencester coach stop, for our goodbyes.

As we waited for the bus, I secretly wondered if I should be leaving him with his limp, his inserted metal, his fake, manmade hip and his stick. Was I being mean and selfish? Peter has always been a very practical, non-emotional person and I'm sure he saw it for how it was: just ten days away. I saw it as if I was abandoning him in his hour of need. As I've said before, we're so different. Anyway, as the bus approached, we hugged and I pretended that I was FINE. I got onto the bus, which was packed and waved wanly to him, as we drove away.

I sat next to a a young girl who slept the entire way to the airport. She didn't open her eyes once. Was she hung-over, exhausted or pretending?

I'll never know, but I wished I could be *her*.

#

Peter claims there's no such thing as jet-lag. There might not be in *his* life, but there's certainly such a thing in *mine*. Anyhow, how does he explain that the grandchildren's sleep patterns are hugely disrupted by a long-haul flight?

He glosses over this, when asked.

Eleven brutal hours later, I emerged in San Francisco International, feeling disorientated. I'd been in a tin can for eternity, but it was only three hours later in my new world. I'm sorry, but I find that confusing.

It had, in fact, been a good flight, despite the fact I was sitting next to a large woman, who spread herself all over me, in a deeply unpleasant fashion. The seats were even narrower than normal and the back of the seat in front of me felt as if it was inches from my face. Despite all this, for some reason, I actually slept for a while; all the tension of the build-up had obviously got to me and the eye mask and noise-reducing headphones, definitely helped. I'd downloaded things to watch on my phone and I binge-watched the entire series on Netflix of *One Day*. The emotional roller-coaster of Dexter and Emma's relationship kept me well and truly occupied with its *will they/won't they* life.

Spoiler alert: *she dies.*

Getting through American security is always interesting. As I emerged into the huge hall, I saw the meandering backward and forwards of a queue that looked at least two hundred people long. I thanked God I didn't have young children with me and duly joined the 'foreign/alien' passport line and read my

Kindle, as I shuffled forward. It crawled at an ailing snail's pace and when I eventually got to the end of it, after about an hour or so, I was made to feel guilty for even stepping foot in the US. I think they must employ people who genuinely hate all humans. He looked at me and my passport with utter contempt, asking me why I wanted to come to the US. I was tempted to say, *I've got a drug deal to finalise* ... but thought he wouldn't find it very funny.

My ten days with the family flew by, as I knew it would. As I'd been before, I was content to simply *hang out* with them and enjoy seeing the children's school for the first time, collecting them, going to playgrounds and sampling the delights of local coffeeshops *and* Easy Breezy, the children's favourite place, where you get to make your own ice creams and choose your own sprinkles. It turns out you don't have to be four or seven, to enjoy this activity.

Seeing them as a family, made me look back to when we were in our forties with our three children. At a similar time in our life, we also had to uproot and go abroad, but it was very different for us: we had a ready-made 'family' of the Air Force, to help us settle into our new life in Cyprus. My daughter and family had really had to do it by themselves and it had proved difficult, even though the language was the same (two countries divided by a common language and all that). It made me nostalgic for those chaotic times when there doesn't seem time to do anything properly; those times when you're permanently playing catch-up with the house, the admin, your clothes, your hair, your friends, your sleep ... your life. Time with young children is so ridiculously full-on: trying simply to get them ready for school is a mission: *'Have you done your teeth, hair? Have you got your packed lunch? Find your shoes ... get your coat on ...'* and that's before 7.30 in the morning.

In America, collection time is even earlier than in the UK. I remember thinking that three o'clock was too early here, but there, it's often one o'clock and then you have the whole afternoon to deal with. So, then it's on to art club, soccer academy, ballet lessons, gymnastics ... the possibilities are endless, but in San Francisco, there's the driving around the city, the negotiating of every side turning that has to be stopped for and every pedestrian that has to be given away to. There's also the driverless cars to be frightened of – a weird phenomenon that doesn't lend itself to peaceful driving, along with the trams that look like trains, that rumble along the roads. It's all very stop/start and slow – until you get on the freeways where all caution is forgotten; you need your wits about you as people swerve in front of you to get off the freeway, while children are shouting in the back seats.

It reminded me of a time when our kids were small and I got stopped by the police for going over the speed limit through a village; my response: *Sorry, I wasn't concentrating with all this noise in the back*, didn't go down particularly well.

Although I hanker for those days, at the same time, I know I wouldn't be able to hack the noise and chaos any more. It's fine for a visit but ... as a retired couple, you get so used to silence, stillness and peace, that it comes as a shock to the senses. Kids are so full of *life* from the moment they wake up, until the second they're at last asleep. If they're not drawing or learning to read, they're building dens, bouncing on sofas, running along pavements, hanging from bars in the playground, shouting, crying or laughing. The only time there is any respite is when they thankfully ask to watch some TV and then you're wracked with guilt because you feel it's a cop-out, that mindlessly staring at Peppa Pig is not what they should be doing ... but sometimes, everyone has to be allowed to chill out, sit back and for a short while, be quiet. The fact that they may be watching it upside down, doing a headstand on the sofa, is by the by. They're quiet, that's the main thing. I can so remember two of mine watching TV on their heads; nothing changes.

Now, of course, there is the added problem of the internet; at least when our three were small, the only distraction was the TV. Now there are so many extra things for children to do on iPads, rationing time on them has become part of the pattern of motherhood. In some ways, life has become easier, in that iPads can go on long car or plane journeys, to keep the little darlings occupied, but trying to explain to a four year old that they can't continue playing on it all day, can be challenging.

I got a glimpse of real American culture while I was there – everyone was very worked up about the Super Bowl Final, as San Francisco was in it. I was invited, along with the family, to some friends' house to watch it; there was also a kids' party going on at the same time, so noise and chaos was part of the day there too. I sat and watched, trying to understand the game and failing miserably. When I got back to the UK, I innocently said to Peter that it seemed quite similar to rugby and I was met with an icy stare.

"It's *nothing* like it," he said, as if I'd just said something punishable by death.

I persevered.

"But it's the same ball, the same running and touchdowns, the same goal kicks," I ventured.

"Look, you don't understand sport."

"Excuse me?"

"It's totally different."

I couldn't be bothered to continue this conversation. I'd merely pointed out that they seemed to be *roughly* trying to achieve the same things, but, I grant you, with fancy headgear, big shoulder pads, a smaller ball and so much stopping and starting, it took twenty-five minutes to do two minutes' worth of play.

Peter was right in that both games go over my head, but it was fun trying to understand it with a bunch of Americans, who didn't seem to understand it, either. They were all so friendly and positive and took an interest in me, even though I was just their friend's mum. Some people may think Americans are a bit superficial and over-enthusiastic, but I don't. I think we see them from our own sarcastic, negative, understated ... and very *British* way. We are very different people. Americans are more straightforward and I personally like their positivity, especially when it comes to dealing with children. Who wouldn't have liked to have positive feedback as a child, instead of *Could Try Harder* written at the end of a lot of school work? Americans are more prone to praise and telling the kids to have *a wonderful, wonderful day* at the morning assembly, instead of telling them off for some minor misdemeanour.

I discovered that everyone was more interested in Taylor Swift being in the audience than the game itself. Her current boyfriend is one of the players and all the kids (and a lot of the adults) seemed to be riveted. I didn't know much about her before my visit; I'd heard a few of her upbeat songs but, during my stay, I became a big fan. My daughter and kids were major fans and I watched a documentary with them about her and became hooked. Her album 'Folklore' has become one of my favourites; I'd had no idea what a great lyricist she was and what good stories she could tell with her songs. If you're reading this and thinking, for God's sake, you're a seventy year old woman, I ask you to listen to 'Folklore' before dissing my choices. At least three of her songs would definitely be on my Desert Island Disc list.

Having said all that, being a Swiftie is not something Peter's going to aspire to.

#

San Francisco is such a city of contrasts: the highest density of millionaires (and probably billionaires) in the world, yet there are streets full of sad people without anything. I don't want to get all political …but it doesn't seem right. If they wanted to do something about it, they surely could?

We drove down one particular street, not far from the tourist area, where the words *Zombie Apocalypse* came to mind. I found myself staring in disbelief at the bedraggled groups of people who looked as if they'd lost all hope. Since I've come back, I've tried to describe the scene to English friends and they often say, *Well, it's pretty bad here too, isn't it?* But … and this is a big *but* … it doesn't compare. In America, if you have nothing, you really have *nothing*. There is no one who is going to come round and give you a mug of soup or offer you a bed for the night. You are on your own … with your rags, your fentanyl habit, your urine-soaked blankets and shopping trolley full of rubbish. One young guy staggered towards the car and I saw his face full on – ashen white, staring eyes, sores, as thin as a skull. I wonder if he's even alive now. They tend to congregate in certain areas of the city, so it's easy to forget this problem if you live in a good area … but it's both scary and sad to see.

The other face of the city is the stupendous bay, with the Golden Gate Bridge and the Bay Bridge striding magnificently across the Pacific; the wonderful architecture; the incredible food and coffee shops; the huge Golden Gate park with its expanse of green and its Academy of Sciences, its museum and Japanese Tea Gardens. Then there are the quirky names of areas: Nob Hill; The Castro (where, if you're lucky, you might see a naked man with only a sock on his willy); Russian Hill; the Mission; the Tenderloin … and then Twin Peaks, with a view across the city to die for. It's a vibrant, exciting and confusing place. I love it, despite its problems. The trip only served to show me what a quiet life I now live, tucked away in rural Wiltshire, without a driverless car, a drug addled homeless person or a naked man, in sight.

I was sad to leave them all out there, the flight home emphasising how many miles there are between us. When we went off to Cyprus, my poor mum must have gone through exactly this too; that emptiness of knowing your children have other lives to live and that you're nothing to do with that any more. You wouldn't want it any other way, but it's still difficult to reconcile yourself to. If only they were round the corner … if only … if only the grandchildren were at the local school … if only we could babysit now and again. Before the days of air travel and cars, you knew that your family would always be near. Maybe that was awful for the young people, knowing there was no escape? It feels now that so many people end up living in other countries that perhaps it's a choice – to fly away, to see new things. Who am I to say that's wrong? I did it myself ... following my man and his job to foreign climes, leaving my mother to fend for herself. It must have been a lot worse for her, as she was alone.

At least Peter and I have got each other.

CHAPTER 18

"And isn't it pretty to think, All along there was some invisible string, tying me to you?" – Taylor Swift's song Invisible String

Till Death Us Do Part

And so, that's me, up to date, in March 2024. And that's us. What does it all mean, this life that we've had together for so long? And what's love got to do with it, as Tina would say? The more I think about marriage, the more mysterious and weird it seems. It's such a big 'ask' to expect two people to live together in harmony for so long. When we met, we were mere children, but we *thought* we were grown up. Were we even capable of knowing what we were letting ourselves in for?

I used the quote above for this chapter, as when I heard Taylor's song, it really hit a nerve with me. I have pictures of us both as babies and it's such a lovely concept to think that all along, there was this invisible string tying us together, that we knew nothing about. I know it's romantic and maybe a bit weird, but how else can you explain it? There was Peter, born in December, 1950 ... and me, in January, 1953; two babies born into families living miles apart at the time, but some sort of force drew us together, dragging us from Wembley and Chelmsford towards Guildford in Surrey, where they were destined to meet and tie the knot in that invisible string.

We had a church wedding; in those days, that's what people did. I don't think it occurred to us to have a civil ceremony. Neither of us were particularly religious; I'd had any real faith drained out of me at school with their interminable services and prayers. But still, it was important to have the ceremony in a church, for some reason.

I look back at pictures of that day and wonder why on earth I chose the outfit I was in. How can I describe it? Edwardian lady chic, is a polite term. I remember not wanting a traditional veil and floaty dress, so opted for a hat and a long dress, without a train. I went shopping for the material with a friend and I can honestly say, I bought the material *she* liked; I'm hopeless at making decisions, but you'd think for something as important as my wedding dress, I'd make a choice based on what *I* liked. Being a people-pleaser has so many consequences. But no – the reams of white material (which I now think looks like nice tablecloth fabric) were duly measured out and purchased. My sister was going to make the dress which, now I look back, was no mean feat and a huge responsibility. I've still got the hat (squashed) and the dress (yellowed and crumpled) in a cupboard somewhere. Quite why I've kept it, I'm not sure: a lasting testament to my lack of fashion sense, perhaps.

Peter and his best man wore top hat and tails. I reckon only really posh people wear them now, but in those days, a lot of 'common people' wore them too. I look at our faded wedding photos and I see this thin, chiselled, cheeky chap standing there; he looks about sixteen and I look positively matronly in my outfit. It looks as if some serious cradle-snatching is going on.

August, 1976 was extremely hot. In the south and south-west of England, several places recorded over 330 hours of sunshine, exceeding the previous highest total for August, of 325 hours in Guernsey, in 1899. We got married on 14th August and the day was predictably, blisteringly hot. The ceremony was in Guildford at 12 noon, so the sun was at its peak. Peter and his best man were late ... surprise, surprise. They'd been in the pub, right up until the last minute.

Being me, I wasn't looking forward to being the centre of attention and found the service and vows etc. embarrassing, rather than affirming. My hat had some netting that came down over my face and at a vital moment during the service, a wasp thought it would be amusing to crawl up it, slowly. I wanted to run round the church like a mad woman, swatting it viciously, but I managed to restrain myself and just patted it demurely. I was 'given away' by my best friend's father, as my own father was absent. His stand-in was a remarkably good-looking man, who looked a bit like a glamorous film-star on the day. It's only now that I've realised this; at the time, he was just my friend's dad.

The reception was held in a school a few miles away from the church. The school belonged to some friends of my stand-in dad; it had lovely grounds and some of the photos of the day are of me, sitting casually on the ground in the shade of a large oak tree. I don't, to be honest, remember much about it. I know my mum provided all the food via her job; she worked at a cordon bleu cookery school and she managed to organise all the spare food to be collected together for the day. It was excellent food, but I do remember Peter's mother being horrified that we were having a buffet. She wanted her *'knees under the table'* but we insisted on the more informal option.

There was a lull between the reception and the evening shenanigans. We'd arranged for all 'the young ones' to meet at the *Good Night Club* in Farnham and we all danced the night away there. I definitely remember the incident of the 'crotchless panties'. What on earth was that, you might ask? Peter's best man thought it would be hilarious to give these to me as a present, on the night. I innocently opened the package in front of everyone that evening, not realising what they were. I was absolutely mortified when I saw them; I was such an innocent back then and really didn't find it funny at all. Everyone else did, though and had great fun laughing at me. I've never quite forgotten that.

At the time, we had quite a trendy car: an old Sunbeam Alpine, in bright, metallic blue. When it was time to leave, we were waved off, with the top cover off as it was so hot, with tin cans and 'Just Married' on the back. Funny old thing, but it was *me* who had to drive all the way to London that night. Having been up at the crack of dawn, I was exhausted by this time and can remember hardly being able to change gears. The groom was far too drunk to drive.

We spent our first night together at the RAF Club in the centre of London. I expect we just fell asleep, but I honestly don't remember. It wasn't as if it was our first night together (even though I pretended to my mum it was). We were up next day to fly to Tenerife for our honeymoon and the beginning of our married life together.

If I got married today, I wouldn't do any of the things we did then. It would be a small civil ceremony, a few friends and family for a meal and not much else. It seems that the more you spend on the day, the quicker you get divorced, these days. It's all *Hello Magazine* photos, hundreds of people, castles and Michelin-starred food. The fact that two people are getting married gets lost, amidst the foreign hen and stag do's that cost your guests a year's salary to attend; the 'favours' and the exotic honeymoons in the Maldives, which you've asked your guests to pay for, as you've been living together for five years and have everything you need for the house. Rant over.

Let's take a look at the vows we made to each other:

I, Sarah, take you, Peter, to be my husband, to have and to hold from this day forward, for better, for worse, for richer, for poorer, in sickness and in health, to love and to cherish, till death us do part, according to God's holy law. In the presence of God I make this vow.

I wonder what *having* and *holding* actually means? We've certainly been with each other through *all* the above. We were poor in the sense that the Air Force pay was worse than being a dustman at the beginning of Peter's career and it meant that we drove old bangers that were held together with the eponymous Chappie tins on the exhaust pipe. We *were* able to buy houses though, unlike the current generation of renters, but the mortgage was a huge part of the salary. At one point, when we had two children and I was pregnant, I remember Peter cycling for an hour each way to get to work, as we couldn't afford a second car. First world problems, I suppose.

I've touched on the sicknesses we've both had; we've certainly loved each other … but not sure about the cherishing part.

We're getting ever nearer the *till death us do part* part now and I don't like it one little bit. Humans have a wonderful capacity to ignore the fact that we will definitely die someday and one day in the future, or maybe even today, if I walk out and go under the proverbial bus, I'll cease to be. It's hard to get your head around. If I'm lucky, there might be a gravestone somewhere in the future with my name on it and a date.

Sarah Knights, Born 30th January, 1953. Died: (?) *Sometime soon, unfortunately.*

I like these more modern vows that I found on the internet and I think they sum up what I've tried to describe in this memoir.

The Way You Are

I promise to accept you the way you are. I fell in love with your qualities, quirks and outlook on life. I promise to respect you as a person with your interests, desires and needs and to realise that those are sometimes different, but no less important, than my own. I promise to join with you and to share all that is to come, to give and to receive, to speak and to listen. I will work by your side with kindness, honesty and trust to create a wonderful life together.

Two very different people, coming together forever and creating a life together, is never going to be an easy thing to achieve. There have always got to be compromises in order to 'keep the peace'. If one person in the relationship is always the one who gives in, or changes, it's not going to work. If neither do, that's never even going to get off the starting blocks. But changing doesn't mean changing *who you are;* it means adapting to someone else's needs or wants and them doing the same for you.

To accept you the way you are is probably the most important vow there is. The other person isn't going to change their personality, just because they've got married. *They are who they've always been.* I think when we were younger, there was a lot of resistance to compromise on both sides, but as we've grown older, we've come to realise that it's the *only* way forward. You either want to stay together, or you don't ... and if you're going to be together, it's often going to be hard. But you somehow get through the hard parts, the arguments, the tears, the disappointments ... because you know you're better together.

Another modern vow:

I Choose You

Three words are stronger than I love you. Today, I stand before you to say, 'I choose you'. I choose you over all others. I choose you to share happiness with. I choose you to care for. I choose you to have a family with. I choose you to grow with.

I choose you to love forever.

I have chosen and been chosen. However randomly it happened ... that day at a tennis club when he asked my friend for a light and I answered the phone when they all rang me ... it was the catalyst for a lifelong friendship, the beginning of our love story, the birth of our children and fifty years together. We're better together, however hard it is.

And do you know what? We *still* laugh at each

other's jokes.

THE END

www.sarahcatherineknights.com

If you enjoyed this memoir, how about reading one of Sarah's other books?
See on the following pages.

BOOKS BY THIS AUTHOR

Aphrodite's Child (Book 1 Of The Aphrodite Trilogy)

Will a new life on a beautiful Greek island lead to the end of a seemingly perfect marriage?

Emily, a mother of two, dreamt of having a third child. When she joins her husband on Cyprus at the beginning of the nineties, she hopes that she can persuade Luke that three children will make their family complete. Little does she know that Luke has been lying to her about their future.

It takes her a while to adjust to her new life, but as she grows in confidence, she begins to love the island. She embraces new experiences, makes new friends and re-discovers herself. A chance encounter with a handsome, single man, however, thrusts her down a dangerous road and her life begins to spiral out of control. Her dreams of getting pregnant never fade but when she eventually finds out about Luke's deceit, their marriage seems doomed.

A tragedy within their friends' circle puts her own dilemma into perspective and makes her realise that she's lost all sense. Can she rescue her marriage or will her actions mean that her family will never be the same again?

This is a story of secrets and impossible choices. Set against the stunning backdrop of sun-soaked Cyprus, you too will fall in love with Aphrodite's island and be captivated by this gripping family drama.

Now Is All There Is (Book 2 Of The Aphrodite Trilogy)

Can her husband, Luke, ever forgive her for what she's done?
In the captivating sequel to 'Aphrodite's Child', Emily returns to Cyprus, hoping for her life to be restored, but her world has been turned upside down. Luke is cold and distant with her, her best friends have gone and she feels utterly lost. The ghosts of the past collide with her uncertain future. Amidst this chaos, Emily encounters Beth, a fellow wife of an airman, whose own existence teeters on the brink of disaster. The two women forge an extraordinary connection, uniting in their shared struggle. Together, they begin to envision a brighter future.

Emily hopes her old life will be re-established when she goes back to England for good, but Luke's unexpected posting to Cornwall leads her to make one of the biggest decisions of her life and this pushes her down a road that can only end in tragedy. Despite the choices that have brought her to this point, Luke's enduring love for her becomes a beacon of hope. He battles desperately to rescue Emily from the depths of her own self-destruction, yearning for her to find redemption and reclaim her true self. 'Now Is All There Is' will leave you breathless as you witness the unfolding of the next chapter in Emily's story.

The concluding part of the Aphrodite Trilogy,'Shadows in the Rock'will be a must read.

Shadows In The Rock (Book 3 Of The Aphrodite Trilogy)

Will Emily's daughter ever come to terms with her parents' past?

In the captivating, final book of The Aphrodite Trilogy, the story follows the path of Emily's daughter, Abi, as she embarks on adulthood. The dark shadows of her parents' past have always haunted her and she's desperate to leave home and break free. She moves to London, convinced that she wants to be independent and embarks on a career as a fashion photographer. But her new life turns out to be far more difficult than she ever imagined.

When she has to accompany her boss on a shoot to Cyprus, she jumps at the chance to see the place that has dominated her parents' lives and her very existence. While there, she experiences both the worst and the best that life can offer. She is forced to grow up quickly and face life head on.

Can she learn to love herself and forgive her parents or will she follow her mother's journey of self-destruction?

'Shadows in the Rock' is the concluding part of the Blackwell family saga, which brings everything together in an emotional, satisfying finale.

Life Happens (Book 1 Of The Life Series)

She's loved him since university ... but he married one of her best friends.

Rachel has always been the beautiful outsider, the one who yearns to have the handsome husband and the perfect family. But she let the love of her life slip through her fingers at university and now happiness is always just out of reach.

She marries an Air Force officer on the rebound and lives on military camps, but she feels like a fish out of water. When her husband takes early retirement, she begins to live again, starting her own business and finding her independence. But when they goes on holiday to Cyprus with her two best friends and their husbands, secrets and lies begin to emerge which will change her life and the lives of everyone she holds dear, forever.

She must now face up to her past and confront her new present. Will her marriage and her friendships survive? Will she ever find true happiness?

'Life Happens' is about the powerful bond between three women and one woman's enduring love. If you enjoy women's fiction set on a beautiful, sun-drenched island with plenty of emotional complexity, you'll love this first book of the 'Life Series'.

Life's Complicated (Book 2 Of The Life Series)

In the sequel to the ever-popular novel 'Life Happens,' Rachel, Jen, and Grace must confront a question that haunts us all: Can you ever truly know someone?

The three women have been inseparable since the eighties, but their recent momentous holiday in Cyprus has left them reeling. As they return home and try to pick up the pieces, they realise that their trip has set in motion a series of events that will affect their lives forever.

Rachel is single again, Jen's health is in jeopardy and Grace embarks on a new chapter in her life. As they navigate their way through these challenges, Rachel's sons, George and Harry and Jen's daughter, Amber, become entangled in their parents' struggles. But time marches inevitably onwards towards the global pandemic and they must all face the two extremes of life: birth and death ... and everything in between.

Will Rachel find her happy-ever-after or does she have to spend the rest of her life, wondering 'what if'?

'Life's Complicated' is an emotional rollercoaster and a powerful testament to the strength of friendship and how it can define us all. Set in Brighton and London, the drama eventually returns to Cyprus, where it all began.

Love Is A State Of Mind

What would you do if, after years of what you thought was a happy marriage, your husband suddenly announced he was leaving you for good?

Anna is in her fifties and is living a contented life. Their children have left home and she and her husband work at the same school. One day, a perfectly ordinary day (or so she thought) they are sitting on a bench during a walk with their beloved Labrador and David drops a devastating bombshell: he's fallen in love with a colleague and is leaving her.

At first, she wants to hide herself away, but, with

the help of her friend and her daughter, she realises that there has to be life after a long marriage; she must move forward. She makes some huge changes: she leaves her job, moves house and goes to visit her estranged sister in Australia. As she navigates her new life as a single woman again, she discovers she's stronger than she realised.

Can she build a new life, find new love and a 'happy-ever-after' or will she be on her own forever?

If you love humorous and poignant novels about women facing up to the harsh realities of life, then you'll love this emotional and uplifting story.

Marvellous Mabel And Her Amazing Ball (Children's Book)

Can Mabel change her behaviour, with the help of a group of friends?

Marvellous Mabel, a lovable Labrador, is obsessed by her amazing ball. It's her favourite thing in the world. But it's becoming a problem, because she can't think about anything else.
When George, a wise old police dog, suggests she joins the VOA group (Various Obsessions Anonymous), Mabel meets a friendly mix of dog friends with crazy obsessions of their own: there's Biggles, the squirrel chaser; Queenie, the food thief; Doris, the hole digger and Boris, the letter snatcher.

Through this heartwarming tale, they must all learn the magic of balancing their addictions to find true contentment.

'Marvellous Mabel and her Amazing Ball' is a story that celebrates how a problem can be much easier to solve with the help of others. You can find happiness together - you just have to ask for help.

Printed in Great Britain
by Amazon